Who is John Dawes?
(And Why Should You Buy Th~~is Book?~~)

John Dawes is an independent Internet consultant and found
online resources, like MusicPromotion.net. He is most known
Internet music promotion on GetSigned.com, where he has e
how to effectively promote their music on the Internet. Over the last few ye~~ars~~
helped record labels, artists and songwriters develop their online personas. He has con~~tinued~~
champion independent artists through online chat "lectures," talk radio, and seminars.

Who is Tim Sweeney?

Besides the fact that you have seen his name mentioned in hundreds of articles and while Tim
is one of the most talked about people in the music industry, it still may not be clear to you who
he is.

To put it simply, Tim Sweeney is one of the music industry's most highly sought after experts
and consultant in the fields of artist development, record company development, distribution,
radio promotion, publicity and retail marketing. His career in the industry spans from his days
as an artist to almost every position at various major labels, to becoming the President of a
successful management company, to becoming the author of some of the music industry's Best
Selling books and audio workshops.

Over the last 18 years, he has helped several major labels (Columbia, Epic, MCA, Warner
Bros., Capitol, Mercury, BMG and Polygram) develop the careers of some of their most promising
and successful artists of all time. Tim has personally developed the careers of more than 1,500
artists to date.

His workshops alone are attended by more than 10,000 artists, musicians, songwriters,
managers, and label Presidents every year. His books alone are used by some of the most
prestigious universities in the United States and are read and used by independent artists in 27
countries around the world.

Now, in this book, John Dawes with Tim Sweeney, will teach you what you really need to
know about putting your music online and promoting it to further your career. You'll learn:
getting music on the Internet and protecting it; how to get airplay on Internet radio, what a
successful Web site should look like; marketing a site online and offline; how to get free advertising
and exposure online and offline; how to write promotional material; the secrets to preparing and
submitting your site to all of the major search engines; and how to grow a Web site's traffic and
keep fans interested.

Who This Book Is For

If you're thinking about starting your own indie label and you want to learn how to overcome the obstacles you'll face in getting your music online – this book is for you.

If you're an independent artist and you want to make a career of releasing your own music online – this book is for you.

If you're an artist, musician, or a songwriter signed to a major or independent label – this book is for you.

If you're an artist manager and you want to learn how to develop the online presence of your artists, so they can reach the broadest possible audience with their music – this book is for you.

If you're a music writer, or even a music fan, and you want to better understand what it is that artists and record labels have to go through in order to bring you the music you hear online – this book is for you.

The Complete Guide to
INTERNET PROMOTION
for Musicians, Artists, & Songwriters

By John Dawes & Tim Sweeney

Published by: Tim Sweeney & Associates
31805 Highway 79 South PMB 551
Temecula, CA 92592
Tel: (909) 303-9506
Fax: (909) 303-9507
www.tsamusic.com

Attention Colleges and Universities, Corporations, and Professional Organizations: Quantity discounts are available on both purchases of this book for educational, training or gift giving purposes. Special booklets or book excerpts can also be created to fit your specific needs. For information, contact the Marketing Department of Tim Sweeney & Associates at the address above.

Notice of Liability
The information in this book is distributed on an "as is" basis, without warranty. While every precaution has been taken in the preparation of this book, neither the authors nor Tim Sweeney & Associates shall have any liability to any person or entity with respect to any loss or damage caused or alleged to be caused directly or indirectly by the information contained in this book.

ISBN 1-929378-01-7

Printed and Bound in the U.S.A.

Foreword

The battle for the Internet has officially begun! Actually it has been a scattered skirmish for years. Nowadays, you can't turn on your television without seeing at least one or two "dot com" commercials every half an hour. Everybody and their dog (literally), seems to have a web site. They are trolling in "the sea" of the Internet, hoping to catch customers as they supposedly go "surfing" by. Since people have been "fishing" for years, in the lakes and oceans of business, they have always had the grand illusions of catching the "big one." That's where we come in.

The Complete Guide to Internet Promotion for Musicians, Artists and Songwriters takes one thing into account. *Reality.* This book is based in reality.

As you know, I have been asked by thousands of artists over the years, to create new books and audio workshops that would actually help artists, musicians and songwriters like yourself, create strategic marketing plans, see real sales of their own CDs and reach their goals for their music career. With the success of my other books and audio workshops, it was time to address the issue that has been affecting the mind set of almost everyone participating in the music industry. How am I going to make the Internet really work for me?

That is the question that I face in my email and over the phone every day. Fortunately, I found someone who was already effectively addressing that issue. John Dawes, my co-author and Internet music consultant, has been helping artists and songwriters for years. With the combining of our two philosophies in the 1990's, we have seen artists, musicians and songwriters realize their goals of understanding how the internet really works. We have actually watched them get paid for their CD sales and merchandise from their own web site and through other retailers on the Internet.

Make no mistake about it. This book is revolutionary. It is completely different than others. We have painstakingly written out a step by step plan that will actually help you succeed on the Internet. We have covered every issue and question we could possibly think of.

How do I know this book is different and for that matter, better? Simply because I have read every other book regarding music and the Internet. Believe me when I say, that I could not find another book that provided you the information you *actually need* to be successful.

As with my other books, it doesn't mean others won't try to copy us and our philosophy, like I have seen with my traditional promotional methods over the years. It just means that others will eventually realize that to be successful on the Internet, you have to redesign and combine your current off-line marketing campaign with your new on-line promotion.

So without further delay, do the following. Sit down in a quiet place, clear your mind of all the "junk" you have heard about the internet and be ready to learn how you are going to actually make the internet work for you.

Tim Sweeney

Table of Contents

Introduction

For the first time, the Internet is leveling the playing field between big corporate bands and the independent musician. The fact that any musician can reach a global audience, get noticed by the industry, and sell their own music proves that the Internet is fundamental to success. The Internet provides the independent artist with the opportunity to play and sell music to a new audience of music fans all over the world, twenty-four hours a day, everyday of the year. This was unheard of only a few years ago, as the recording industry monopolized every other channel of distribution for decades.

As a result, the Internet has left the door wide open for the independent artist. Yet, most are overwhelmed by this opportunity. This is where *The Complete Guide to Internet Promotion for Musicians, Artists, and Songwriters* (CGIP) comes in. CGIP is the first book to contain a comprehensive plan to help you and your music get on the Internet and have verifiable success. This book will also show you proven techniques in promoting and distributing your own music through the Internet. By the final page you will know how to get online, increase your fan base, sell music, and get more advertising for little or no money.

CGIP maps out the order of steps to a successful online promotion campaign and covers *in detail* the most important elements of promoting yourself online *and* offline. Here's how. CGIP contains five sections: *Creating a Strong Online Presence, Promoting Your Web Site Offline, Promoting Your Web Site Online, Creating Online & Offline Publicity for Your Music*, and *Online Issues*.

The first half of section one, *Creating a Strong Online Presence*, will familiarize you with the various types of Internet Service Providers; how to choose the best one for your budget; what kind of computer system you will need to put your music online; and where you can learn more about the technical side of the Internet.

The first section will also help you define an overall strategy, using all of the sections in this book. It also provides you with the formula for an eye-catching layout and some basic design tips that will make your site stand out (the most overlooked aspect in a web campaign.) By the end of the first section, you will know which obstacles to avoid and how to turn them into your advantage.

Once all of your materials are in order and your site is ready, section two, *Promoting Your Web Site Offline*, explains how to get the most out of marketing and promoting your music offline, just like the pros. Section three, *Promoting Your Web Site Online*, teaches you how to coordinate your offline promotion campaign with your web site.

The fourth section, *Generating Online & Offline Publicity For Your Music*, raises the ante by discussing more ways to gain free exposure for you and your music. It will also show you how to make your music available to the masses digitally; the newest methods to selling your music without making a CD; how to handle the different phases of online growth; and how to maintain a strong online presence while moving with the tides of change.

Finally, section five covers the *Online Issues* that concern artists today and emerging technologies that will benefit the independent artist. These include the burgeoning on-line legal scene, how to protect your music online, and how to ensure that your copy rights are not unreasonably taken.

No matter what your level of experience, CGIP's purpose is to empower you and your music and to provide you with an in depth understanding of the strategies you will need to move your career farther than before. With that in mind let's get started!

Sincerely,
John Dawes.
IndiePromo.com

Email: info@indiepromo.com
Web: http://www.indiepromo.com
Address: P.O. Box 500202, San Diego, CA 92150

PS: Be sure to visit our web site frequently - www.indiepromo.com - for the latest tips on music promotion, updates to chapters, and more independent music resources. If you still have any questions about how to get up and running or improve your existing site, don't hesitate to contact us. We offer expert consulting and web design services. See the coupon in the back of the book for a great deal! Remember, your purchase of this book entitles you to a free membership to our artist development center. How to get your personal access code is at the back of the book.

SECTION I

Creating a Strong Online Presence

CHAPTER 1

Creating an Overall Strategy

As you know, the Internet is constantly evolving and presenting something new everyday. So the real trick is how to get online and consistently stand out from the crowd. To put it simply, you must have a plan of attack in order to successfully promote yourself online. While there isn't an exact formula for success, this chapter will teach you how to spot online trends and exploit them.

Most importantly, *Creating an Overall Strategy* sets the pace for using your local offline promotion (word-of-mouth, gigs, and press coverage) to open niche markets online (email lists, newsgroups, search engines, ezines, Internet radio, online vendors, distributors, etc.). But before we begin exploring the finer details, it is absolutely paramount that you understand that your efforts online are *not* independent from your efforts offline.

Cyber-Artists Need Not Apply

It is easy to get caught up in all the hype about the Internet and immediately start thinking of getting global exposure. With a bit of planning, an independent artist can grow from a local scene, expand into niche markets and onward to the global scale. While traditional methods of promotion translate easily into the online realm, there are completely new methods you need to take advantage of. Even though the Internet is one of the cheapest ways to get exposure, it is important to understand that traditional methods of promotion are still valid and integral to your success. This is because the Internet is merely a new medium, not a departure from the "old ways."

Lesson: **Online promotion should never replace offline promotion. Instead, the two should be used together in a synergy, one complementing the other**.

Again, before delving into the gory details of getting online and selling music, let's walk through an overall strategy that will help you build a stronger online presence. Most of this strategy is a natural extension of the offline promotion you are already doing.

Plan of Attack

A web site is like a business. It must be carefully planned and executed to measure its success. With a well-developed plan, you will be able to analyze the elements that are responsible for causing your promotional campaign to fall short or become a smashing success. Here are the five key points to developing your overall plan and the chapters in this book that cover them:

- **Getting Your Act Together**
  Deep Thoughts: Do *you have finished, mastered songs and a finished CD? Do you know your market? Have you gathered all your information?*

- **Securing Your Online Presence**
  Chapters: *Online Basics & Putting Your Music Online, How to Become a Multimedia Dynamo,* and *Elements of a Successful Web Site*

- **How to Integrate Your Web Site with Your Offline Promotion**
  Chapters: *Starting a Propaganda Machine, Using the Press To Your Advantage, Using Email Effectively*

- **Using Your Online Presence to Leverage More Exposure**
  Chapters: *Understanding Search Engines, Submitting to Search Engines, To Yahoo! or Not to Yahoo!, Internet Radio & Online Publicity, Where Does the Money Come From?,* and *CyberPrise: Thinking E-Commerce.*

- **Cultivating Growth and Longevity**
  Chapters: *Covering Your Bases, Measuring Your Success, Protecting Music Online,* and *CyberLaw.*

Getting Your Act Together

Now that you are ready to get your music online or even if you already have some kind of online presence, you need to make sure that your image is polished. That means having well produced songs and a finished CD to sell as your main "product." You will also need to create a press kit or convert your existing one to your web site. *Elements of a Successful Web Site* will explore this and show you how to design your site to have the most impact for your intended audience – fans, the press, and industry professionals.

Securing Your Online Presence

The first step in creating an online presence is to get connected to the Internet and begin searching for a place to put your web site. *Online Basics & Putting Your Music Online* covers in detail where to find the best places to store a web site based on need; how to pick a web address; and how much all of this will cost you.

The next step is to start building your site. *Elements of a Successful Web Site* and *How to Become a Multimedia Dynamo* show you what your site should contain and how to organize it for the most impact. Note: this book is not a tutorial in web design. Unfortunately, web site design is a subject for an entire book, but don't worry. If you are a "do-it-yourselfer," there are online resources where you can learn web site design listed throughout this book.

Securing your online presence is the largest step but not the most difficult. There is a great deal of work involved with building a new web site and announcing its grand opening. If you don't own a computer or know the first thing about web design, don't let that stop you from getting online. There is always somebody around to help. (A geeky third-cousin, perhaps? See first coupon in the back of the book.)

To start you off in the right direction visit Newbie-U at http://www.newbie-u.com to learn more about the Internet and basic concepts of networks; how to use any of the popular web browsers, email and news reader programs; and where to get your hands on useful file utilities. With WYSIWYG (What You See Is What You Get) web page editors, there isn't much to learn about HTML anymore. These nifty editors take care a lot of the tedious programming work for you. Many of the popular WYSIWYG web page editors are available on a trial basis. See the table on the next page to find the best one that works for you. Also, be sure to visit the CGIP web site – **http://IndiePromo.com** - for more useful tutorials and online education.

When taking on designing your own web site, keep one thing in mind. You get what you pay for. Also, if you have a "friend of a friend" maintain your site, it will be difficult to get any changes made in a timely manner and it will look like a "friend" maintains your site, instead of a professional public relations firm. Many of my new clients' web sites are repair jobs because they are victims of amateur web masters.

Integrating Your Web Site with Offline Promotion

While you are building your web site or having it done for you, start tagging all of your merchandise and literature with your email and web address. I can't tell you how many times I have seen this overlooked. Most of the artists that I meet at lectures complain how a single soul has never visited their site. I have found that a majority of them do not put their online contact information on business cards, CD's and merchandise. On the other side of the coin, make sure the web address you want isn't already taken before printing up cards and CD jackets!

When your site is fully functional, announce it to the local press with a news release and inform existing fans through email and snail mail. You can increase interest by holding a contest or making a special offer to encourage people to visit your site - something like, "Order a CD from our new web page and get a free sticker and T-shirt. Offer limited to the first one hundred." The word "free" will have a huge draw, while "limited offer" adds a sense of urgency.

Notice how search engine submissions are not part of this step! This is because a new artist site will get more results from the "word of mouth" than from search engines. Your time is better spent using other techniques to draw visitors that are more likely to buy your CD because they are familiar with your work. This is called "product recognition" in marketing circles and will lead to stronger sales. The next point of the overall strategy covers the first part of the online gamut.

Leveraging More Exposure

At this stage of your online presence, your site should be fully integrated with your offline promotion. Your existing fan base knows about your web site and can give you invaluable input on its effectiveness. With their help, you can "fine tune" your online presence in preparation for the global scene. You are now ready to conquer search engines and to begin submitting your music to Ezines, reviewers, Internet radio, and online "music stores."

Understanding Search Engines and *Submitting to Search Engines* teach you how to optimize your web pages for all of the major search engines. *Internet Radio & Online Publicity, Where Does The Money Come From?*, and *Cyberprise: Thinking E-Commerce* will show you how to use your web site to leverage more exposure and increase CD sales.

However, even after your online promotion kicks in, a majority of traffic will still come from word of mouth. A client of mine received 12,000 hits from word of mouth alone, before I submitted her new site to search engines. Those hits came from 400 plus visitors listening to all of her music, exploring the site thoroughly and interacting with band members. The reaction to her new site was a direct result of mentioning her site during gigs while on tour, putting it on flyers, imprinting it on CD's, and including it in press releases. Imagine what would have happened if my client submitted her site to CD Reviewers, Ezines, MP3 sites, and Internet Radio, too!

Cultivating Growth and Longevity in the Global Scene

This is the easiest part of the overall strategy. When traffic starts to die down at your site or you want to go to the next level of intensity, *Covering Your Bases* and *Measuring*

Your Success will show you how to attract new fans and keep long-term interest in existing ones. All you have to do is spend just a few hours a month following the methods outlined in the chapters above and search for more ezines, reviewers, online "music stores," and Internet radio stations to place your songs. Resources like these pop up everyday so there is always a way to generate interest in your music. Spending just one hour a week finding new resources will make a huge difference in the traffic passing through your site. To help you keep track of your progress, a checklist is at the end of each chapter, starting with chapter 3. For your convenience, *Appendix A* contains a comprehensive checklist.

Keeping Track of Your Progress

We realize that the Internet is constantly changing and it is impossible to keep this book up to date as soon as it is on the shelf. To ensure that you have access to the latest tips and techniques, Tim and I have put together a companion web site for CGIP - **http://IndiePromo.com**. There you can get updates to chapters in this book, the comprehensive checklist, tutorials, more study materials, software, online resources, and advice to help you develop your music career. All you have to do is come visit us at: **http://IndiePromo.com/updates**. You also get a limited-time free membership to our "Indie Insider" section. See the coupon at the back of this book to get your personal access code.

CHAPTER 2

Online Basics & Putting Your Music Online

It has never been easier to gain an online presence. Anyone with the smallest effort can build a web site. That's why it is more important than ever for your site to stand out among the masses. During the course of this book, we will explore various ways to ensure your online longevity, by giving you a strong foundation to build your online presence.

Whether or not you are new to the Internet, this chapter will put the technical aspects of building a web site into perspective. It will also familiarize you with the everyday "language" of a professional "web master." Vocabulary is half the battle and being able to speak the "language" will empower you to communicate with other web masters, fans, A&R reps, and the press. This will go a long way in your being taken seriously and getting exposure.

In addition, we will show you how to plan your online promotion campaign, what it will cost you and most importantly, how to make money from it. However, before we explore the aspects of getting your music online, let's take a brief look at *how* your web site will be an effective promotional tool and what it *should* do for your career.

What a Web Site Should Do For Your Music Career

Simply put, a web site is another "tool" to be used in building your music career. Most of our clients, as a direct result of their web site, have seen an increase in sales, higher attendance at concerts, and a stronger interest by A&R reps. Their success can be attributed to integrating their offline promotion with their web site and keeping fans informed with regular announcements. They also have a strong "community feeling" on their web site. Throughout this book we will show you how to do all of this and more. Even with all of the methods in this book, a *plan* is essential to the success of your web site, and thus, your music career. But before we can get into the techniques of promoting a web site, let's take a quick look at what you need to get started.

What You Will Need to Get Started

Getting connected to the Internet and setting up a web site can seem overwhelming. So we have put this section together to smooth out the bumps for you. *Even if you already have an Internet connection and a web site set up, read this section carefully.* Besides all of the technical mumbo-jumbo, this section will show you how to save money getting online, what factors can harm your online promotion campaign, and what the various types of services can and can't do for you. All of which will help you build a strong online presence. With that in mind, consider the following questions:

- Which computer system will I need and how do I connect it to the Internet?
- Where will I house my web page?
- How much room will I need for my web pages and audio files?
- Who will build my web site?
- How do I get my music to play from my web site?
- How much service and support will I get from my Internet Service Provider?
- How do I accept credit cards?
- What will all of this cost me?

Which Computer System You Will Need

The most difficult decision most people have to make when buying a new computer is deciding between which brand; IBM compatible or Macintosh? In the old days, Macintosh's ruled the music world with hardware and software. Today, music hardware manufactures make their products compatible for both systems. The major difference between the IBM and Macintosh is in the software used to manipulate your music and which "look-and-feel" you prefer. Either way, understand the most important features of what the computer will be used for.

My coauthor has always been a Macintosh supporter. The choice is for you to make. Personally, I prefer IBM compatible systems because the parts have always been less expensive to upgrade. Software and hardware for creating music on an IBM compatible is now plentiful. Plus, the Internet tends to be IBM centric because a large majority of the personal computers connected to the Internet are IBM compatibles. This is not to say that the Internet is lacking a Macintosh presence. The Internet is, no doubt, a wellspring of free resources to explore and experiment with for all computer systems.

Whether you decide on an IBM or a Macintosh, make sure that your purchase comes with some kind of a warranty or service agreement. Try to purchase a computer in your local area so that it will be a relatively painless process to get it serviced if something should fail. Talk with the store about in home repair. No matter which computer brand you choose to purchase, you can find reliable systems for under $1000 dollars. If you already have a computer and an Internet connection, you can get started for as little as $70.

Connecting Your Computer to the Internet and Setting Up a Web Site

These days almost any computer system you buy comes out of the box with Internet access. Many of these systems connect to the Internet via an Online Service – i.e. America Online (AOL), CompuServe and free services like NetZero. Even though you may be connected to the Internet, you will still need to find a well-suited Web Host Provider (WHP) to "house" or store your web site.

A Web Host Provider is a company that provides space on a computer connected to the Internet to "house" your web site. There are four basic types of Web Host Providers and they each meet different needs:

- Online Services – provide Internet access and some provide web space
    - AOL, CompuServe, NetZero, and Prodigy

- Internet Service Providers (ISP) – provide Internet access and web space
    - They can be found in the Yellow Pages of your phone book. See *Internet Resources.*
    - Local Area / Homegrown / Small Companies

- Standalone Web Host Providers (WHP) – no Internet access, just web space
    - They can be found on the Internet with a bit of research. See *Internet Resources.*
    - Local Area / Homegrown / Small Companies

- Free Hosting Services – no Internet access, just web space
    - GeoCities, Tripod, AngelFire, XOOM, and SimpleNet

Understanding the Various Internet Services

Now that you are familiar with the different ways you can connect to the Internet and where to erect your new web site, let's explore the best option for fostering a successful online promotion campaign. To start, I recommend that you use a local ISP with a separate standalone Web Host Provider (WHP). Even though your local ISP can provide you with web space, you can save a tremendous amount of money over the long term by using separate services to connect your computer to the Internet for housing your web site. Here is how:

Step1: Find a Local ISP

A local ISP will typically provide **unlimited** Internet access for $10 to $20 a month. This is an important factor because, you will be using your Internet connection to build a web site, to do research, monitor your progress, and promote yourself. You will also have access to local area newsgroups, resources and opportunities that would normally not be available through Online Services.

While Online Services can provide you with web space, they are mainly in business to sell Internet access for "surfing" the web – meandering from web page to web page without any intent or purpose - and reading email. Their sites are notoriously slow and their interfaces are extremely bandwidth hungry. **Essentially, the web space they provide is for hobbyists**.

You can easily find a local ISP in the Yellow Pages under "Internet" or ask someone you know which online service they use and if they recommend it. If you still can not find a local ISP, visit The List at **http://thelist.internet.com**. There you can search for an ISP in your area.

Once you have a satisfactory connection, I suggest that you visit the Newbie-U web site at: **http://www.newbie-u.com**. There you can learn about web browsers, email, newsgroups and all of the important utilities that go along with accessing them. Now we are almost ready to find a standalone WHP. But first, let's think about what web address works best for your music because this is a crucial part of creating a new account.

Step 2: Register a Virtual Domain Name or "Domain Name"

The importance of getting a virtual domain name – http://www.yourband.com – can not be stressed enough. With your own domain, you will have a matching email address to go with your web site – theband@yourband.com. In addition, your site will be easier to remember and stand out from the rest. In the upcoming chapters, we will explore other important reasons why you need a virtual domain name.

As noted in the table on the next page, registering a virtual domain name will cost you $70 for the first two years and then $35 per year thereafter. The process is painless because most host providers take care of the registration for you. All you have to do is check to see if the address you want is available – Visit **http://www.networksolutions.com** to check. When you find the name you want, the host provider will ask you what domain name you want when you sign up.

A virtual domain is the single most important piece of "real estate" on the Internet. *If you are thinking that $70 is a lot of money, consider how much money you will lose because fans won't be able to remember your web or email address.* Don't be a tightwad and sell yourself short. Now let's stake out your piece of land on the Internet.

Step 3: Find a standalone Web Host Provider

Standalone WHPs are the most cost-effective way to put your music on the Internet. You get a lot more speed, space, and functionality for the same money than if you have your local ISP host your web site, too. Standalone WHPs can provide you with the 50 to 150MB of web space you *will* need, as opposed to ISPs and Online Services providing 10 to 30MB in the same price range. This is why **standalone Web Host Providers are a better value than ISP's and Online Services.**

You should expect to pay around $10 a month for a *non-virtual* domain and $20 to $30 for a *virtual* domain, in addition to an initial setup fee. A *non-virtual* domain is a web address that is merely an extension to the host provider's domain name – i.e. **http://www.hostprovidername.com/yourbandname**. *Virtual* domain names allow you to "brand" your site with your name – i.e. **http://www.yourbandname.com**. However, there are additional fees to register your site with a virtual domain name. See the table on the next page for typical hosting fees.

STANDALONE WHPs ARE YOUR BEST BET

- **At Least 50MB Storage Space**
- **Unlimited Traffic**
- **Forms and Scripts**
- **Secure Transactions (SSL)**
- **Audio / Video Streaming Server**

Contact MusicPromotion.net to get a great deal on web hosting and web site design together. See what they have to offer at: **http://MusicPromotion.net/webhosting**. Their packages are specially designed to meet the needs of online musicians like yourself - tons of space and dedicated RealAudio servers. You can also find more places to search for standalone web host providers in *Internet Resources*, but before you make any decisions, you will need to find out how much space you will need.

What You Should Expect to Pay for a Web Host Provider

	Non-Virtual	*Virtual Domain Name*
Web Host Setup Fee	$0 to $35	$0 to $35 + $70 Registration Fee
Web Host Monthly Fee	$5 to $20 / month	$15 to $35 / month

Be aware that many of the smaller web host providers may charge an arm and a leg to add more space as your site grows, so shop around.

How Much Space Your Site Will Need

It is important to anticipate how much space your entire site will need before you finally select any WHP. This is because audio files will take up the most space. Even with the best compression technology, a band page with a few sound files and a couple of photos will barely fit in 30MB of web space. To give you a rough idea of how much web space you will need and again, why WHPs are your best bet, let's look at how much space your music files take.

A typical three-minute CD track can be squeezed into a near CD quality 4MB MP3 file. For example, let's say you released an LP that only has eight songs and you wanted to put the full length of each song on your site. Already you will need 32MB of web space. In combination with RealAudio, which will squeeze the same CD track down to about 150KB, another 1MB (8 tracks x 150KB = 1.2MB) will be needed.

Now with graphics and web documents, you will need an additional 1 to 5MB, depending on how many photos and press clipping you have. You will also need room for your statistics log (keeps track of where surfers are

Units of Measure Used in Data Storage and Bandwidth

MB = 1 Million Bytes = 1 megabyte
KB = 1000 Bytes = 100 times smaller than a megabyte

coming from), guest book, order page and incoming email. Already you have exceeded 38MB in need and we haven't even considered any other CDs or video files in your discography. If your site runs out of space then it could cease to function properly!

> **Bandwidth** is used to describe how much data can pass through a wire, i.e. how much water can pass through a water hose. The thinner the hose, the longer it takes to transfer a gallon of water, no matter how long the hose is and if the pressure is kept constant.

Although you can get started with an Online Service, we recommend that you find a local Internet Service Provider (ISP). Basically, ISP's are faster; provide better email management; allow you to choose the Internet utilities and web browsers that work best for you; and offer personalized customer service. Best of all, **ISPs give you ultimate control over promoting your site**.

Online Services, like AOL and NetZero, are popular because they make it simple to setup an Internet connection. However, there is a hefty price to pay. Online services are slow and force you to suffer through a pile of advertisements.

Online Services and ISP's not only connect your computer through your modem to the Internet and the World Wide Web but they can also provide web space. However, this is not the case for standalone WHPs and free web providers, as they do not provide any connections to the Internet for your computer. It is strongly recommended that you avoid *free* services, like GeoCities, XOOM, etc., for reasons that will be explored in greater detail in the next section.

A Word About "Free" Web Hosting Services...Beware!

A surefire way to kill your online presence is cutting corners by using free hosting services like GeoCities, Tripod, and XOOM. They place so many obstacles in front of potential fans that you may never sell a single album from your site. Here are four major reasons to avoid using free web sites:

1. Annoying Pop-up Banner Ads.
Non-fee based web providers use the word "FREE" to attract customers, but they display ads that pop up all over your "free" site when fans visit! Plus, they try to offer you more products and services through a barrage of email marketing and

online surveys. Pop-up ads do nothing more than say that you are a tightwad and don't take your music seriously.

2. They are slow.

Free web sites are not optimized to transmit multimedia files and can add unnecessary download time to your site's content. Most visitors will abort their visit to a web site if nothing comes up within the first 9 seconds. A slow web site also means your audio will be "dropping out" or skipping like a scratched CD.

3. The address is too long.

With web addresses becoming a familiar part of the media landscape, it is unreasonable to expect fans to remember web addresses like:

> http://www.geocities.com/Music/Jojo/index.html
> http://www.yourwebhostprovider.com/yourbandname
> http://www.usacollegecampus.edu/~yourloginname
> http://www.mp3.com/yourbandname

Try fitting any one of these on a business card or T-shirt! A web address should be short and simple. As mentioned earlier, your best bets are:

> **www.firstandlastname.com**
>   - or -
> **www.bandname.com**.

Notice there are no slashes(/), tildes(~), or any other terms that have nothing to do with your band name.

Please note that even with a free Web Host Provider, you will still have to pay the $70 domain name registration fee AND up to $30 to set up "forwarding" to your "free" web site. What a waste of time and money! Remember, it costs the same to have a virtual domain name set up, whether you use a free or full-blown megabandwidth web host provider! Plain and simple, invest in a virtual domain name.

4. Search engines ignore them.

Due to the growth of the web in recent years, search engines like, Yahoo!, Alta Vista, and Lycos have had a very difficult time providing useful information to surfers. In an effort to remedy this, **most of the major search engines have chosen to ignore free web sites entirely**. This is because free web sites are associated with "my pet cat" sites, hobbies, and other amateur endeavors. This would explain why your hard work in getting into search engines is not paying off if you already have a site hosted by a free host provider.

To add insult to injury, the purveyors of this plot are themselves providers of FREE Web Sites. Yahoo! maintains GeoCities. Lycos owns Tripod and AngelFire. Ouch!

Additionally, free hosting services do not have the capability to process web forms. These are the interactive and "money making" parts of a site – i.e. guest books, sign-in pages, shopping carts, order forms, etc. This will make it difficult to create a community feeling - more on this later. Plus, email is not provided as part of the service. Although you can get a free email account from the many popular search engines, like Yahoo! and Microsoft Network, you will start to spread yourself thin with a web address dissimilar to your email address.

By using a free web site, you have very little control over how fast you can grow your exposure, modify your image, experiment with new technology, and test new marketing ideas. Even if you are diligently promoting offline and online, your efforts will be entirely in vain because your site will not be able to handle the traffic. However, if you have absolutely zero capital and free hosting services are the only way to get started, you will have to build your online presence and then *move* your site to a better host provider.

Local Area Directories and Meta Sites, Another Free Site Pitfall

Almost every city has a music scene publication. Many of these are publishing on the web and providing free listings - usually a single page with a bio, some songs, and a web link. You could take advantage of this service but do not use it as your "official" site. Mainly because it will be difficult to get the web master to update your events calendar or any other information about you and your music in a timely manner. Again, it will be difficult to stand out among the masses.

The same goes for Meta Sites like MP3.com, Internet Underground Music Archive (IUMA), and the Ultimate Band List (UBL). Do not use them as the hub of your promotion campaign! You won't be able to grab the spotlight with thousands of other acts under the same web address – i.e. http://mp3.com/ralphmongers and http://iuma.com/ralphmongers. You also won't have control over the content and *personality* of your page. You can also bet that these services are plastering ads above your "free" site.

It is extremely important to have your own site in addition to using Local Area Directories and Meta Sites. *Understand that these services are only a means of letting people know you're out there and where to find you, much like an ad in the Yellow Pages.* In *Promoting Your Web Site Online* we will explore more venues of free publicity that are worthwhile.

Final Thought: FREE is a Four-Letter Word...Sometimes

With the advent of FREE Web hosting services, it has never been easier to gain an online presence. Anyone with the smallest effort can now erect a web site. That is why it is more important than ever for your site to stand out among the masses and avoid the distractions caused by having a FREE Web Host Provider.

In addition to annoying ads, speed deprivation and an unoriginal domain name, a FREE web site guarantees that you will be ignored by search engines and unheard by fans. No matter how you slice it, you are loosing money if your site is on a FREE provider. Don't waste any more of your time with them if you are serious about your music career.

Finally, do not Band-Aid together a bunch of free services like web hosting, email, and Meta Sites to achieve an online presence. Instead, use them in conjunction with an "official site" that has a personality of its own. In order to have a successful web campaign, you need to have complete control over a web site that has its own virtual domain name on a standalone Web Host Provider. With all of that in mind the next chapter, *Elements of a Successful Web Site,* explores how to begin with a strong online presence by building an effective web site.

CHAPTER 3

Elements of a Successful Web Site

Now that we have an ISP and a stand-alone Web Host Provider, with a domain name, let's take the next step to creating a strong online presence with your web site. Every aspect of a successful web site centers on creating a "community" feeling. By that we mean adding a personal touch to your site, where visitors feel at home. Achieving this is where design and layout of your site become a crucial part of its success. We want our new and existing fans to feel a bond with us, as artists, and our music so they will constantly return to our web site. **The key element to creating an effective online community is interactivity. As you build your site, ask yourself, how easy have you made it for fans to reach you.** To make sure you accomplish this, let's begin with the basics you will need.

Getting Your Act Together Before Building a Web Site

Your next step is one of the most important in developing your web site. Ask yourself the following questions, "Do I have finished and mastered songs?", "How about a finished CD?", "What image am I trying to present?", and "What is my audience?" While some of these may be difficult questions to ask, it is important for you to have the answers. Otherwise, getting your music online is a complete waste of time - not to mention trying to succeed with it offline. If you already have a press kit, some photos, and a finished CD or collection of recorded and mastered songs, you are ready to get started online! But before you jump ahead, let's explore each question to see where you are.

Do I have finished and mastered songs? A finished CD?

Putting your music online means you have to be "radio ready." You should have a finished CD with artwork and a proper UPC barcode. The reasons for this are:

- Web-based audio file formats accentuate the effects of tape hiss and other sources of studio noise. Your CD will have these removed in the mastering process.

- Without a CD, you will not have a finished product for people to buy and you to profit from.

- Most retailers require a proper UPC barcode be filed with the UCC as a means of accounting and inventory control.

- If you're interested in a record deal in the future, you won't have a strong representation of your work for visiting A&R reps and other industry people to review.

It will certainly help to have a finished product but you can get started without one. However, this is *strongly* discouraged. Again, using a demo quality recording may turn off potential fans to your music and disappoint A&R reps. If you decide to go forward anyway, it would be in your best interest to **clearly identify any demo material on your site.**

What is My Image? Audience?

If you are still struggling to find your image or audience, visit the web sites of your musical influences or other successful groups and observe their layout. After identifying your target audience, create a mood to match your image along with a distinctive logo. If you're on a limited budget, it is feasible to use your album cover instead. You can learn a great deal from others. Ask web designers for tips, as they like to share their success stories and experience. By keeping all of this in mind, you will start marketing your site to the right audience.

Image is Everything

The look and feel of your web site should mirror your musical style. An effective use of color along with the right mood can reinforce a passerby to stop and look around for awhile. Remember that marketability applies to the web just as it does to CDs. Identifying your audience will be extremely helpful in the design and layout of your site and will help create the all important "community" feeling. Once you have an idea of what personality your site will have, you will have to convert your offline press kit to the web. It is a *vital* part of keeping your group in public view.

Online Press Kit

Before designing or discussing your new site with a web designer, gather all of your personal information. Review your biography and press releases, gather press clippings and reviews, and compile your discography. Carefully read them. You will want to consider how accurately they represent you and your music and whether they need to be updated or rewritten. You may be able to pass off some of this work with first drafts to a web designer that specializes in package deals - highly recommended.

Converting your press kit into its "cyber" counterpart is a relatively easy matter. However, creating a press kit from scratch can be a large undertaking. If you haven't put together a strong kit or have neglected your current one, then this section will help you get things in order. To start, a press kit must be kept up to date and contain the following:

- Press Release(s)
- Biography
- Press Clippings / Reviews
- Professional Photos
- Discography / Time Line
- Booking Information
- Up-to-date Events Calendar and News

> Return your investment by including your web site on a Hybrid CD - a.k.a CD-Extra. Multimedia CDs are emerging as a powerful form of promotion. Everywhere your music goes, so does your press kit.

Press Release

A well-drafted press release can get you free advertising. Send it to every applicable music magazine you can find along with an event calendar. Word your release in a way that will make the editor feel like he/she is benefiting their readers by publishing it. *Starting a Propaganda Machine* will cover how to author and distribute press releases online effectively.

Quotes-Press Clippings

Quotes and clippings are a great way to show you are legitimate. **Don't go overboard and include everything that makes mention of you in your kit.** Use only your best clippings. If you don't have any reviews or write-ups, you will have to generate them by sending out press releases and albums for review. (See *Internet Radio & Online Publicity*.) When quoting part of an article, credit the publication, not the author. Each clipping and quote should have a date. Consider removing old quotes and articles after a few months. If you haven't been getting reviews for several months, you can keep your façade up by just removing the dates and keeping the articles. Just keep in mind, that outdated clippings will make information on your site appear stale. Most importantly, make sure you have the publication's permission to put their article, write-up, review, etc. on your web site!

Bio

A bio tells your story. It can describe the creative process and familiarize potential fans and industry reps with your history, musical style, and aspirations. A bio goes a long way in adding a personal touch to your press kit and web site. There are many different writing styles used in bios. However, one point to remember when writing yours is to avoid opening phrases like, "At the age of 5, my mom had me take guitar lessons. By 9 years of age, she knew I was better than the Beatles. By 12..."

Gig Calendar

A calendar will make it easy for fans and A&R reps to find you. Keep it updated and delete dates more than a week old. Nothing will kill return visits to a web site more than outdated and useless information. A huge plus with fans would be providing directions or a map to gigs, and a phone number where they can buy tickets or contact the venue. You can really "yuck" it up with A&R reps by listing all venues and events performed in on a separate page, along with your booking information.

Discography

Include all of your releases, even singles or projects with other bands in your kit. Potential fans of your music will be impressed by your sizable discography and existing fans may want to know if they have all of your work.

Something to watch out for: putting all of your album covers online can add unnecessary download time to your site. A stylish way around this is to use *thumbnails*. A thumbnail is a reduction of an image that, when clicked on, will load the original photograph to full-size and resolution. Every visitor, with a fast or slow connection, will then have the freedom to choose the viewing size of all your album covers.

Guest Book

Anything that increases communication between you and your fans increases the community feeling. The simplest form of interactivity can come in a sign-in page or guest book. Fans can give valuable input on your music and web site. Plus, you can build a large contact list by collecting names, locations, and email addresses.

Newsletter / Email

Email is one of the great benefits of the Internet. Building a large email list will pay off because it will enable "back door" promotion of newsletters, gigs, short notice items, and new music. Sending regular email updates is key to longevity online and offline because fans will always be aware of your progress. In addition, email lists are more cost effective than *snail mail* because email is instantaneous and costs almost nothing. If a gig is canceled or changed at the last minute, fans can be notified instantly.

Whether it's new fans, visitors to your site, or A&R reps, all of them are frustrated by artists' web sites where they can't find the email link. Make sure that your email address is visible on the front page of your site. More ways to use email effectively are covered in *Using Email Effectively*.

Regular Updates Keep Fans Happy

Keep your press kit current. Any dates older than six months will show that you are inactive. Web surfers have come to demand current information. They simply won't return to your site if it has stale events, reviews, or press clippings. You don't have to change your entire site, just keep dates current and any news in a visible area. Encourage fans to give you their email address so that you can notify them of any updates or events. In addition, state when the next update will occur at the bottom of your home page.

Elements That Make Your Site Better

So far we've really only talked about web content. While content is one of the most important parts of your site, let's explore what you can do to enhance the presentation or layout of your site. This section will help you to remove any further obstacles from fans buying your CD, contacting you, and spreading the word of mouth about your music. All of this entails selling your CDs direct to fans, audio file enhancements and other multimedia gimmicks.

You've Got Nothing to Hide

A web site should be intuitive - easy to use - and communicate its content at first glance. Visitors should know instantly where to hear and buy your music, where to read your biography and reviews, how to contact you, sign-in, etc. Essentially, your site must create a mood or have a personality of its own and be an extension of you. This is often referred to as the *wow* factor.

While you want your site to have an artistic flare and its content to *sizzle*, you also don't want to hurt your fan's eyes with extreme colors, lots of animation, and backgrounds that make the text difficult to read. Keep your site as simple as possible and choose your color theme carefully. The objective is to visually interest your fans, but more importantly, let the text and your music communicate the message.

Common Design Mistakes

- Dark backgrounds with dark text
- Light backgrounds with light text
- "Busy" backgrounds
- Huge graphic files
- No audio and video streaming
- Non-intuitive interface
- Poor spelling and grammar
- Excessive Animation and Java
- Dead Links!

Basic Web Site Architecture: Simple is Better

Since your site will be fulfilling different needs, let's talk a little about how a web site should be laid out. The best way to address this is, consider who will be visiting your site:

- Local Fans
- International Fans & Fans Abroad
- A&R Reps
- Local Press
- International Press
- Stray Visitors & New Fans

We have a long list of different people with completely different expectations! So how do we build a web site that can meet all of their needs and interests? Simple...section off your site into web pages for each group and promote them independently. Let's examine the demand of each group:

- **Local Fans:** This group most likely owns your CD. They are mainly interested in any new developments: gigs, music, news, etc. You will need to provide a calendar and some points of interest on a separate page. Make sure you include an address, time, and contact info for each venue. Your discography will also enforce their need to own all of your work. In *Internet Radio & Online Publicity*, we will explore more ways to attract more fans abroad.

- **International Fans & Fans Abroad:** These are fans you want to attract to your site to buy a CD. They are not likely to attend concerts unless you tour abroad. Again, points of interest and new developments will need to be emphasized. Most importantly for this group, make sure it is clear how to order your CD and how to listen to your music samples on *every* page of the site, especially your home page.

- **A&R Reps:** You want this group to learn about your success and consider your music as a product available for acquisition. They shouldn't have to go through the process of purchasing a CD. Consider offering your CD and offline press kit to them for free. A&R Reps will also want to keep track of your progress, especially if they like what they see AND hear. You will need an "artist profile" page with links to audio files separate from the regular page that just serves as a listing of your work. This page is well suited for radio station managers, DJs, as well as the press.

- **Local Press & Press Abroad:** These folks are not likely to visit your site unless you are already considered newsworthy. So you will have to go to them. *Starting a Propaganda Machine* will cover this in detail, but for now, how your site is organized will make it easier for them to publicize you when, they do drop by. You will need a media kit to provide materials for print and online media. This is separate from the A&R "profile" page.

- **Stray Visitors & New Fans:** These folks are just passing through and have either found you on another site from "surfing" or from the word of mouth. You have to do everything possible to convert them into fans. Your site will do all the talking here and will have to "scream" at them to stay and look around for awhile. Without a compelling mood, stray visitors will just keep on going. Typically a "splash" or introduction page with your logo or a distinctive photograph, will set the mood for the rest of their exploration of your site.

So there you have it. This is what the audience of a music-oriented site boils down to. The same goes for the sites of songwriters, promoters, labels, agents, and managers. In addition to the pages that are optimized for the different audiences above, you will need the standard bio, gig calendar, audio, and contact pages. The figure on the next page is a site map to give you an idea of the simplest and most effective web site *architecture* - the way the pages are linked together.

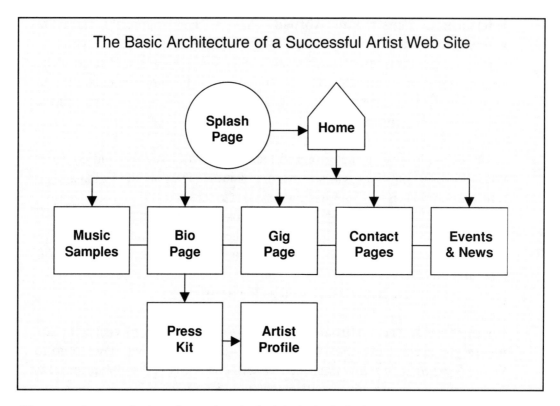

The Basic Architecture of a Successful Artist Web Site

You may be wondering about the circle labeled "Splash Page." This is an introductory page, that should have your logo or a high-quality picture that sets the mood of your site and music. It's an introduction to your potential fans' *experience* of your site. The Splash page is also another way to put short-notice items on your site and to promote new events, contests, giveaways, and drawings.

Also, notice in the figure above that the Artist Profile and Press Kit are separate from the rest of the site – a "dead end" from the Bio page. Even though the Artist Profile and Press Kit contain some of the same basic information, they are "optimized" for the intended audience. This will allow you to focus a separate marketing effort towards A&R Reps and the Media, without your fans having to navigate through information they don't necessarily want or need.

As you are reviewing your current bio and press kit and decide that you want to have information that will set you above other artists, consider developing an Artist Profile and converting it onto your web site. If you don't know what an Artist Profile is, call **Tim Sweeney** at **(909) 303-9506** and pick up a copy of *The Living Room Sessions by Tim Sweeney,* or visit the CGIP companion site to order online: **http://IndiePromo.com/pubs**.

Streaming Audio

One of the main purposes of a web site is to allow visitors to "sample the product" before buying it. Unfortunately, many artists avoid the web entirely because they fear theft and copyright violation of their work. (See *Protecting Music Online*.) A simple fact of "music life" is that if you want to sell more CDs, then you need to put your music online. While there are many ways to put your music online, the most popular option is RealAudio. It is free, easy to implement, and it supports video. With software available for download, one can convert and compress audio or video to a "web-friendly" format in minutes.

Once your music files are web-friendly, you can *stream* them from your site. Streaming allows surfers to experience a site's multimedia content while it is being transferred or "dowloaded." This is a great feature that many sites overlook, forcing their visitors to wait for an entire file to download for several minutes before hearing or seeing anything. The faster visitors can access your music, the better. Unfortunately, there is a sacrifice to streaming multimedia files. The audio and video quality is not pristine and for that reason alone, many "purists" are strongly against using RealAudio. However, the compromise in audio quality is outweighed by making more music accessible in a shorter amount of time. Besides, if fans want the best audio quality possible they should buy your CD.

By skimping a little on audio quality and song length, you can encourage visitors to support you. Fortunately, there are a multitude of ways that you can make your music available for quick review and at the same time available for download in a high quality format that would make any audiophile happy. We will explore this subject in greater detail in later chapters, *CyberPrise, How to Become a Multimedia Dynamo,* and *How to Protect Music Online.*

Video & Web Casting

If you have footage of a live show or a music video, don't be shy. Put it online! This can be a great attraction for new and old fans, alike. It will also increase the community feeling and make your site stand out from the rest. However, keep in mind that including

---

Streaming Audio Formats

RealAudio:
www.realaudio.com

Shockwave:
www.shockwave.com

LiquidAudio:
www.liquidaudio.com

Windows Media:
www.windowsmedia.com

QuickTime3:
quicktime.apple.com

a lengthy video clip will take up a great deal of space on your site and time to download. Unless you use real-time streaming (with RealAudio, WindowsMedia, etc.), your videos will be viewed by only a small percentage of visitors because they will have to download the entire file first.

Singles and Mixes

This is an excellent way to add an air of exclusivity to a web site and spearhead more sales. Perhaps you have live material that was not put on your latest CD. Or maybe you are a long way from releasing your next album and have a few songs completed. Fans would love nothing more than a sneak peak at your latest stuff or even to purchase a download of some new songs.

E-Commerce: Selling CD's Direct to Your Fans

The new buzzword on the Internet is *E-commerce*. That's fine and dandy but what does e-commerce mean? To put it simply, it's electronic commerce or selling products online. However, simple it is not. It's getting online, erecting a web site, promoting it, setting up a store front and order page, processing orders, mailing CD's and merchandise, and…well…you get the idea. It takes a lot of work to fulfill orders but I'm going to show you how you can be lazy and still get paid.

Accepting Credit Cards On Your Own

If you already have a web site, it would be a mistake not to accept credit cards in addition to checks and money orders. It is a proven fact that accepting credit cards increases impulse buys. Processing credit cards is also the most efficient way to collect money and fulfill orders. However, this convenience can come with a heavy price tag.

Card services usually charge higher rates for transactions by nontraditional retailers because they consider them to be "high risk." Primarily, because it is harder for consumers to return product. If you have bad credit, many card services will boast they can finance you. *Don't fall into this trap.* Your transaction fees and financing rates will be substantially higher, making your profit margin shrink a great deal. In addition, if sales do not reach a certain amount each month the major card companies - VISA and MasterCard, especially - charge a "minimum" processing fee to your card service. They gladly pass this fee onto you - the customer.

Unless you sell a large amount of merchandise, accepting credit cards on your own is not economical. Fortunately, there are other options. One can use Internet Billing Services (IBS) to accept credit cards and process orders without a large initial investment. So how does one know where to begin?

What You Need To Process Credit Cards

Whether you will be able to process credit cards on your own is determined by several factors. If you are already selling a lot of merchandise and/or carrying several items (CDs, shirts, stickers, MP3 files, etc.), you should consider processing cards yourself. If you have bad credit, make only a few sales (less than 10 CDs per week), or carry a couple of items, then go with an IBS.

To accept credit cards on your own, you will need a credit card verification service, merchant bank account, order fulfillment (i.e. stuffing your CDs into boxes and shipping them out), and a Web Host Provider that furnishes SSL encryption. For an initial setup fee and a percentage of each sale, an IBS will process credit cards for you. Many "drop ship" or fulfill orders, as well. Here is a detailed examination of what you will need:

Accepting Cards on Your Own
It is necessary to acquire and maintain the following to process credit cards:

- **A Merchant Bank Account**
- **Secured Socket Layer server access (SSL)**
- **Credit Card Verification Service**
- **Shopping Cart Page / Store Front**
- **Order Processing / Tracking**

Pros and Cons
- Cost can vary from a few to several hundred dollars to start off.
- Financing and Insurance required to cover equipment.
- Fees per transaction. (You need to make $1500 to $2000/mo. in sales to break even)
- Special equipment required.
- Need to carry inventory, fulfill orders, shipping & handling.
- Storefront development / Maintenance / SSL.
- Collection of Sales Tax.

Internet Billing Services (IBS)

They do all the work. All you have to do is provide product:

- **Don't need a Merchant Bank Account**
- **Don't need Secured Socket Layer server access (SSL)**
- **No Shopping Cart Page / Store Front Development**
- **No Order Processing / Tracking**

Pros and Cons

- Can cost nothing to small setup fee
- Most carry inventory and drop ship for you
- Larger IBS's require a UPC label (Amazon.com & CDNow)
- Take percentage of each album sold
- Order page doesn't match site's theme
- Breaks professional facade and can be disruptive

An IBS is a tremendous saving of time and money! Until you reach a large volume of sales, this is the only way to go. A great IBS is CD Baby. They drop ship merchandise and don't require a UPC label on your CD. Tell them that Taco Truffles sent you and get a substantial discount. For more information visit **http://www.cdbaby.com**. A list of other reputable IBS's can be found on our site: **http://IndiePromo.com/ecommerce**.

CDNow and Amazon.com offer similar services but can take longer to fulfill orders. They also take a bigger percentage. Plus, you won't get personalized attention. However, the advantage of going with one of the larger guys is that a majority of customers prefer to buy from a huge reputable online vendor. You can cover all the bases and submit materials to each IBS, like diversifying a site in search engines. By the way, another online music store, The Orchard, will carry your CD and handle distributing it to CDNow, Amazon.com, and Music Boulevard for you. They have strict guidelines and won't do this for just any-one. Visit their site to find out more: **http://www.theorchard.com**.

Potential Problems & What to Avoid

As we talked about before, a web designer along with the help of other professionals can give you and your music the best chance to succeed on the web. Let's take a look at some of the potential damage other artists have done to their online presence by being "do it yourselfers."

```
                        Drop Shippers

        CD Baby - http://www.cdbaby.com
        The Orchard  - http://www.theorchard.com
        also distributes your CD through Amazon and CDNow:
        Amazon.com – http://www.amazon.com
        CDNow – http://www.cdnow.com



                    Card Processing Services

        Card Service International - http://www.cardservices.com



                    Internet Billing Services

        CCNow – http://www.ccnow.com
        iBill - http://www.ibill.com
```

Multimedia Pitfalls

Some band sites try to cater to different visitors by providing their music in several web-friendly formats, such as MP3, RealAudio, QuickTime, and Shockwave. While this may seem to be a good idea, it can be an administrative nightmare. I recommend picking a format and sticking with it. However, many artists use RealAudio to demo a song available for download in MP3 format. RealAudio has become the standard for streaming audio because the price can't be beat - free. Plus, most surfers are familiar with RealAudio and already have it installed in their browser. For surfers that don't, it is only a simple matter of providing a link from your web site to RealAudio's download page.

Graphics and Photos

Don't fall into the trap of using amateur photos. Only use professionally taken photographs. Most amateur web designers abuse oversized graphic files and don't take into account that many surfers on the Internet do not have a fast enough connection. Users don't want to wait for large files to download or see full-screen images. Keep photos down to a minimum on your home page and set aside an entire page for a gallery. There are many tools available on the Internet that will allow you to edit and compress images.

Macromedia Fireworks2 is a popular image-editor program that is well suited for optimizing graphics for use on the web. It is available on a trial basis at **http://www.macromedia.com/fireworks**.

Compatibility With The "Other Guys"

WYSIWYG (What You See Is What You Get) web page editors have made it a lot easier to build a web site without knowing a single thing about HTML programming. However, you still have to make sure that your site is compatible with Online Services – AOL and WebTV - and the major web browsers – Internet Explorer 2.0 to 5.0 and Netscape Communicator 2.0 to 4.7. Most editors come with a "site check" feature that will tell you how your site's code will be handled by every version of the popular browsers. For AOL and WebTV, there is no way to ensure your site will function correctly without testing your site through their interfaces.

D.I.Y. Web Kits

Even with WYSIWYG web editors, you still have to keep in mind that web design is more than a technical skill. The Web is a new medium that combines a bit of television, print media, and a heap of direct marketing. The time you will spend learning web design, graphic editing, and multimedia would be better spent on hiring a professional web designer. Before you embark on designing your site, improving it or hiring a web designer, contact **Taco Truffles Media** directly at **(858) 613-1635**. Of course you can contact us through the companion web site at **http://IndiePromo.com/webhelp**.

TIME TO CHECK IN:

Check off all of the materials you already have and make notes on what you need. If you plan to have your site designed by a professional, skip the *Get Online* section and continue on to *Start Thinking About Your Image*:

- **Gather Personal Information**

    ❏ Compile Discography / Time Line

    ❏ Draft Bio
    > Avoid opening phrses like, "At an early age..."

    ❏ Draft Press Release
    > Prepare an announcement for the launching of your web site

    ❏ Gather Press Clippings & Reviews
    > If you don't have Reviews or Clippings, you'll have to send out CDs for review. See *Internet Radio & Online Publicity* for a ton of resources.

    ❏ Compile Gig Information
    > List your recurring gigs first. Then, list ALL of your gigs together. Don't forget directions, contacts, and where to buy tickets!

    ❏ Consider Merchandising
    > Set a budget for T-shirts and stickers, at the very least. You can cut corners on T-shirts buy placing your web address on the left sleeve, instead of the front and back.

- **Get Online**

    ❏ Choose An ISP Based on Need:
    > How much room? (greater than 30MB is ideal)
    > Dial-in Access
    > Service / Customer Support
    > Web Server Features:
    >> 1 Personal Domain Name

2 Interactive Forms (CGI/Perl)
3 Email Account
4 SSL Encryption Server

- Free ISP's do not include features 1, 2, 4, customer service, dial-in access, and provide little space (3 – 10MB)
- Commercial Online Services (AOL, etc.) typically only include features 2, 3, and provide little space.
- Most Web Host Providers include features 1 to 3. 4 is usually extra when available. Try to obtain a provider with at least 50MB housing space.

❏ Find a Web Designer or DIY
Get a Package Deal - Bio, Discography, Web Site Submission, etc.
      - or -
Do It Yourself. You'll need to know:
    HTML Programming
    Multimedia Conversion
    Graphic Design
    FTP / Telnet / Maybe some UNIX
    CGI and Perl scripting for forms
    Web Page Optimization

- **Start Thinking About Your Image**

❏ What Image Do You Want to Present?

❏ Content and Layout?
Photos? Do I have all of the following ready: Bio, Press Release, and Reviews? Interactivity: Sign-In, Order, and Feedback forms? Do I want to publish a news-letter.

❏ Color Scheme?
Avoid using pictures for your background. Only use solid colors. Remember, simple is better.

❏ Logo?

- **Consider Accepting Credit Cards**

  Compare the Cost of the Following Methods:

  ❏ If You Have Good Credit & Sell Tons of Your Music
      Obtain a Merchant Account at a local bank

  ❏ If You Have No / Bad Credit & Are Just Starting Out
      Obtain Internet Billing - CD Baby - www.cdbaby.com

NOTES:

NOTES:

NOTES:

NOTES:

CHAPTER 4

How to Become a Multimedia Dynamo

In this chapter we are going to cover what the different technologies are that enable you to make your music web-friendly, put it online, and what protection each file format affords. While this chapter could easily become an entire book, I will limit this discussion to the most useful file formats and software programs that will get you up and running the quickest. But first, we need to cover some basics.

Multimedia Basics

There are three questions you need to answer that will affect the delivery of multimedia from your web site:

> How fast do you want your music to be heard?
> How much audio quality is necessary to satisfy listeners?
> How much security do you need?

The technology that has been developed to solve these issues:

> **Compression:** Squeezes the audio file to a smaller low fidelity file
> **Streaming:** Fans can listen while music transmits from your web site
> **File IDs:** Segment in audio file that contains info about you
> **Watermarking / Encryption / Dissolving & Expiration:** Security measures to prevent piracy

Unfortunately, because a large majority of Internet connections from the home are at low speeds, a trade-off has to occur. This trade-off is either a high fidelity audio file, which means bigger file sizes and longer delivery times, or real-time playback and lower fidelity audio. This also means that you will have to use several formats to cover the bases – i.e. surfers with fast connections, slow connections, and consumers that demand high fidelity audio. This situation is slowly changing as more homes are provided with other means of connecting to the Internet at high speeds through their cable television companies or Digital Subscriber Lines (DSL). Modems are on the verge of becoming a part of the past.

Take a look at the table below. As you can see, RealAudio uses both compression and streaming to address the first two questions. However, it does not come with any useful security measures without expensive web server hardware. The MP3 format uses compression but is incapable of being streamed in near CD fidelity. It does not come with any security measures either. Liquid Audio provides CD quality audio and built in security measures, but this format can not be streamed from a web site without expensive specialized hardware installed on your web server. *Protecting Your Music Online* covers some very useful methods on how to keep theft of your work to a minimum.

What Each Web-friendly Audio Format Does to Protect Your Music Online

Audio Format	Security	Compression	Expiration	Streaming	ID Information
MP3		✓			✓
Real Audio		✓		✓	✓
Liquid Audio	✓	✓	✓		✓
WAV					✓
Windows Media		✓		✓	✓

As mentioned before, I recommend that you use a low fidelity streaming format to offer a sample (RealAudio) and then offer a higher fidelity file (MP3 or LiquidAudio), either as an up sell or for download. It is entirely up to you. It all depends on what you are willing to give up for some exposure. Now let's take a look at each format and how to create them from your finished CD.

Web-Friendly Music Formats

In order to make your music web-friendly, you have to convert your CD. This process is often referred to as encoding or "ripping." Today, encoding your CD into useful formats, like MP3 and RealAudio, is easy. All you need is a piece of software that will encode each track. There are literally hundreds to choose from and new ones coming out at an astonishing rate.

CD Rippers are simple to use. All you have to do is put your CD into your computer and select the tracks you want to encode, press a button, and wait. Keep in mind that most of the free players record at less than CD quality or allow only a few rips before disabling or "crippling" themselves. You can always download trial or free versions to find the best fit for your needs:

- **RealJukebox – http://www.real.com** from the makers of RealPlayer, is offered in free or "Plus" versions for Windows (US$29.99). The free version records up to 96kbps (128kbps is considered CD quality), versus 320kbps for the Plus. Plays all audio formats and rips CD's to RealAudio, MP3 or WAV. If you already have RealPlayer G2 or RealPlayer Plus G2, you can download a free 2.85MB update.

- **RealProducer – http://www.real.com** also from the makers of RealPlayer and is offered in free or "Plus" versions for Windows or Mac (US$29.99). With RealProducer you can vary the compression for different connection speeds, and for source audio categories – i.e. voice or music. This format can also be used to stream video AND audio. This nifty program will also generate the HTML pages necessary to stream RealAudio and RealVideo files. It also has "Wizards" that step you through the encoding process. An extremely useful tool if you have little or no experience with HTML programming.

- **MusicMatch – http://www.musicmatch.com** for Windows. Like all jukeboxes, this program is an all-in-one digital audio player, recorder and database software program. The basic program is free; but the "CD quality" version costs US$29.99. The free version records only in "near CD quality," up to 96kbps, whereas the commercial version records up to 160kbps.

- **Xing AudioCatalyst – http://www.audiocatalyst.com** is a CD ripper for Windows or Mac. It can also encode WAV files to MP3 (or AIFF to MP3, in the Mac version). The features that come with this program have the professional musician in mind. You can set the start and stop points and normalize the volume levels, so that all your files are at the same volume. It supports from 32 to 320 kbps. A free trial version with limited features is available; full version is US$29.95.

- **RioPort Audio Manager – http://www.rioport.com** is designed by the same people who make the Diamond Rio portable player. This player/CD ripper for PC or Mac includes an MP3 browser and is very fast and easy to use. There is also a facility for loading files into a Rio player. You can download and use it free for the first 50 MP3's. It comes free with the Diamond Rio 500, costs $4.95 with Rio 300 or $9.95 as a stand-alone product. Choose from bit rates ranging from 64 to 256 kbps.

After you have encoded your CD into the various web-friendly formats, the only technical part left is how to make them accessible from your web site. We will start with the format that covers the most bases, RealAudio.

How to Make RealAudio Stream From Your Site

When you want to get the music section of your site started, use RealAudio. The main reason is that it is the fastest way to set up streaming multimedia from your site without expensive hardware and software. While you can easily download RealProducer, it will generate a unique page for each song you encode. It is not recommended to separate your songs. This is because you want every song on one page. Visitors don't want to navigate to every unique song page. Plus, RealProducer plasters banners on the pages it generates.

Instead, just encode your songs to a RealAudio file (.ra) and create what is called a Meta File (.ram). Meta Files are plain text files that contain one line with the URL of RealAudio file itself. Of course, you will have to know where the file will be stored on your web site or server in advance. RealProducer can create Meta Files for you, but it puts the local path name of the .ra file on your computer instead of a valid URL.

For example, let's say that you encoded track one on your CD and called it *funkyjunky.ra*. You know that it will be uploaded in the same directory as your home page – known as the "root." Therefore the URL to *funkyjunky.ra* will be *http://www.yourbandname.com/ funkyjunky.ra*. Before you upload *funkyjunky.ra*, create the Meta File with that URL in it and call *track1.ram*. You can call the Meta file anything as long as it ends in *.ram*. Upload both files to the same location to make it easier to keep track of your audio files.

Now, in order to stream your RealAudio file *funkyjunky.ra*, all you have to do is link your music page to the *track1.ram* file as *http://www.yourbandname.com/track1.ram* – not the .ra file. Voila, that's all there is to it. No fancy hardware or software. Granted this is not a bullet proof method and you may get drop outs during the busiest periods of the day, but you have your music available in an easily accessible and popular format. Here is what the HTML code will look like to link to the *track1.ram* Meta File:

```
<A HREF=http://www.yourbandname.com/track1.ram>Funky Junky (RealAudio)</A>
```

What is that MP3 thing really?

The problem here is that MP3 is a public format. *MP3.com did not create nor holds any patents on this format.* This causes a bit of a problem and confusion. The main problem is that the MP3 format is publicly available, making it hard to find decent software to encode CDs.

When comparing CD rippers, you should pay attention to a specification called *bit rate*, which is expressed as "kbps." This means "kilobits per second," and is a measure of bandwidth or data speed. MP3's use 128kbps as the most common rate. This is considered "CD quality." Without going into too many details, the higher the speed, the better the sound. Think of it like gasoline. The higher the octane, the better the performance. You can use the lower octane, but you will know the difference.

Without a specially dedicated web server, MP3s can not be streamed from your web site, and at that, in mono and less than CD quality. However, it is a simple matter of just uploading your MP3 encoded songs to your site and linking to it directly. For example, the same song on your CD in RealAudio format was encoded to an MP3 file called *funkyjunky.mp3*. You can upload it to the same directory as the other audio files, making its URL *http://www.yourbandname.com/funkyjunky.mp3*. As long as a visitor has any of the hundreds of MP3 players installed on their computers, the rest is handled by the browser. Here is an HTML code snippet:

```
<A HREF=http://www.yourbandname.com/funkyjunky.mp3>Funky Junky (MP3)</A>
```

Titanic Waves in the WAV Format

The WAV format is too big to effectively distribute over the Internet. For every minute of stereo audio it takes a little over 10MB of storage. Since this format does not stream, why bother? There are plenty of other formats for audio purists. Most speakers hooked up to the computer are not high fidelity anyhow. Thus, MP3 and other high fidelity compression formats (Liquid Audio, Windows Media) are more than suited for distribution from your web site. Besides, you don't want to give away the best possible recording of your work because fans could burn their own CDs! They should buy your CD if they want the best fidelity possible.

Other Formats: A Quick Note

Now that you have built experience with RealAudio and the MP3 formats, do some research on other formats. Liquid Audio and Windows Media Files are gaining popularity for various reasons. Keep an eye on them as you may find that you will have to add these formats to your site or even remove others as time marches on, technology improves, and connection speeds increase.

Experience Is Your Best Friend

Because features on these programs change, it is impossible to keep this book up to date. That is why you should visit our web site and take advantage of the free membership that comes with the purchase of this book. More in depth tutorials, specials, and informative articles are available there. See the coupon at the back of this book to get your free personal account.

TIME TO CHECK IN:

Check off all of the materials you already have and make notes on what you need. If you plan to have your site designed by a professional, you can skip this section and move on to the next chapter.

- **Convert Your Press Kit to the Web**

    ❑ Scan Album Covers Into Your Computer
    > If you don't have a scanner, your local copy center will have the facilities to help you.

    ❑ Scan Photos Into Computer
    > Remember, only use professionally take photographs. Pictures taken a gigs by fans or amateurs will detract from you professional facade.

    ❑ Scan Reviews & Clippings Into Computer or Place Quotes
    > Strip your reviews and clippings down to the "bones." No one wants to read the collective writings on your entire career. Highlight the good parts and edit out the rest. One to three lines, with the publication's name, will be plenty.

    ❑ Enter Bio and Press Release into Press Kit Page
    > Don't forget to create a separate optimized page for A&R reps, the press, and your fans.

- **Convert Your CD to Web-Friendly Formats**

    ❑ Download and Install "Ripping" Software on Your Computer
    > RealAudio, MP3 are the most widely used formats online. Review *Web-Friendly Music Formats* to download the appropriate software.

    ❑ Convert your Tracks to MP3 and RealAudio
    > Create Meta Files (.ram) for RealAudio files to take advantage of streaming. See *How to Make RealAudio Stream From Your Site.*

• Put Your Music Files on Your Web Site

❑ "Upload" or Send Your Files To Your Web Site

If you don't know the first thing about transferring files from your computer to your web site, visit Newbie-U to take their tutorial on "FTP" - http://www.newbie-u.com. By the way, FTP stands for File Transfer Protocol.

❑ "Link" To Your Music Files To Your "Audio Samples" Page

Build a web page for your music samples with URLs pointing to each audio file on your web site. Then, upload or "send" the "audio samples" page to your web site.

❑ Test Streaming Audio and Other Formats

Visit your web site's audio samples page and click on the links to make sure that your RealAudio files stream and MP3s download properly. Remember, you need RealPlayer or any MP3 players installed on your computer, in order for sound to work properly from your site. Make sure that visitors are notified which audio formats each URL points to.

NOTES:

NOTES:

Reality Check: Growth on the Internet vs. "Freebie-ism"

The entertainment industry is America's number one export. In addition, music is without a doubt one of the hottest commodities sought after on the Internet. SearchTerms.com has consistently reported that search engine queries for "MP3" is second only to "sex," and has seen "MP3" rank first. This is not surprising, as a large percentage of the population online is in a crucial age group.

Near the end of the last century, more than half of the population between the ages of 16 and 34 in the U.S. and Canada were Internet users. This is the same demographic that makes up the bulk of record industry sales. As a result, the independent artist can reach a large portion of the same market through the Internet that the record industry has dominated for decades.

> A study in September, 1997, by Nielsen Media Research, on E-Commerce showed that the number of Internet users in the U.S. and Canada had reached 79 million, while the number of people buying products and services through the web hit 20 million. As of February 1999, the Internet population has reached 97.1 million and is growing at the rate of 67,000 new users a day. The number of online shoppers has more than roughly doubled to 48 million, as well.

Fighting the Online Freebie Zombies

Don't make the mistake of thinking that with such a large online population that there is a pile of money and opportunity out there. Very few of the original online companies are still in business today because they forgot one important attribute of their online customers. They want it all and they want it for free.

Finding a delicate balance between giving away all of your songs and selling them for the highest bidder is the harshest reality of being online. This has lead to the music industry addressing the issues of piracy and tracking revenue online. In the meantime, many of the methods covered in this book will show you how to convert "Freebie Zombies" into paying fans, by creating a "compelling" mood with your web site.

Promoting Your Web Site Offline

CHAPTER 5

Starting a Propaganda Machine

Many businesspeople are so excited about getting an online business established that, they forget about the real world. Musicians are not any different. They, too, can ail from the myth that as soon as they get online, thousands of surfers will flock to their Web site in a spending frenzy. *Nothing is further from the truth.* As you diligently read this book, you will learn that in addition to the "real world stuff," you have to carefully prepare your site for search engines, make announcements in newsgroups, send email to fans, swap links with other sites, and perhaps join a web ring or two - not to mention all of the hard work in getting your site to pique visitors' interest.

In reality, most of the traffic you will get when starting out is from *networking* with other people. I don't mean networking in the sense of computer communications, but in talking in person to flesh-and-blood human beings. In essence, expanding your current networking efforts. Whenever you talk to your fans or book a gig, you are networking. Anytime you make contact with a person, new or old, talk about your web site! Everything they need to know is on your site and it is always open...right? With that in mind, let's explore more ways to slip your web site into the public consciousness.

Networking

The quickest way to meet people in the music business is to join a local organization and attend meetings. Even if you foolishly believe other members are your direct "competition," they will most likely know someone that can benefit you in some way, shape or form. The types of organizations you will benefit best from are songwriting guilds, musician alliances, small seminars and trade shows. A group that has the interests of the working musician in mind is most lucrative. A list of organizations can be found in the **Yellow Pages of Rock** and **The Recording Industry Sourcebook**. Pick up a copy of each or visit Amazon.com to order.

There are also online equivalents to songwriter and artist guilds that hold regular chats and online events. If you are geographically isolated from any useful organizations, online guilds and artist communities are perfect for your needs. The Muses Muse is one such artist community – **http://www.musesmuse.com**. You can find more useful organizations and communities at Jeff Mallot's Songwriters Site – **http://www.lyricist.com**. Also visit IndiePromo.com for more organizations geared towards specific genres of music – **http://IndiePromo.com/orgs**.

Networking Online with Other Artists and Industry Professionals

Jeff Mallot's Songwriter Site
http://www.lyricist.com

Muses Muse
http://www.musesmuse.com

IndiePromo.com
http://IndiePromo.com/orgs

Concerts

Whenever you perform, pass out a mailing list for potential fans to fill out. Add the option for either an email or mailing address. Many people are more willing to give out an email address rather than their home address because there is more anonymity online. This works in your favor, as it is easier and cheaper to email fans. In addition, pause in the middle of a performance to mention your web address and encourage fans to give you their email address. This will open the door to link swapping later down the road. It is a proven fact that when you are on stage your influence over people is stronger.

Subtle Web Site Promotion At Concerts

Make sure that every band member, roadie, groupie and crew-member knows your web address. This way they won't have to go looking for the one band member that knows the address. Also, encourage your entourage to mention something unique about the site other than, "Yep, its cool. You can download our songs from it." Instead, have them hype it a little, "Our web site is at: …. Check it out. Drop us a line and let us know what you think. We're also giving away free stuff." Remember, benefits, benefits, benefits!

Taking Concerts for Granted

One of the ways I meet new clients is by attending concerts. I usually approach the leader of the group during a break and ask if the group has a web site. The answer is often "yes" and I give my pitch about web promotion. Yet, the leader still fails to mention their site to the audience before, during, or after their gig! Why bother getting online if you don't let people know where they can experience your music anytime they want, sign up for a newsletter, or find out where you're gigging next? Don't make this mistake! Most of the traffic to a new web site comes from mention at gigs. It is important to think locally, first, then work on growing your international online audience. Always take a moment to announce to your web address at every gig! Even try this trick. Have the club stamp everyone's hand with your web address when they enter! Have I got you thinking yet? Looking for more ideas? See the coupon at the back of this book for a copy of **Tim Sweeney's Guide to Successfully Playing Live** or visit IndiePromo.com to cash in the discounts that comes with your purchase of this book: **http://IndiePromo.com/pubs**.

Local Press

Send your press kit, artist profile, or news release to local press and music magazines announcing your presence on the web. A news release should make it clear that fans can get online, listen to music, buy it for cheaper than in stores, and find your latest gig information. It costs nothing to have the newspaper announce your site. New businesses get free advertising like this all the time. This form of free advertising is known as publicity. *Starting a Propaganda Machine* will explore how to write a press release and distribute it in more detail.

Brand Everything You Own

If tattooing your web address on the forehead is not an option, there are still many other possibilities. Change your web address to your middle name, swap email addresses, hand out flyers/postcards, etc. with your address visible. While you are out networking, every album, poster, business card and piece of merchandise that leaves your hand must have your web address imprinted in plain view! Even then, point it out to people. Get your web page to do all of the PR work you can't do while you are not onstage.

www.yadda-yadda.com

Offline promotion is vital to the success of your web site. In addition to literature and the word-of-mouth, it is possible to create interest through merchandise. Here are some ideas beside the infamous T-shirt, key chain, calendar, and coffee mug onslaught:

Contests are a great way to integrate your web site with offline events, like gigs, onetime performances, holidays events, and even launching a tour. A great gift for a contest is a merchandise package (T-Shirts, Stickers, Posters) bundled with a handheld MP3 player. You can even go as far as to program the MP3 player to hold your latest CD or entire song collection. All you have to do is sell 20 to 25 CDs to break even. This is not too hard with a package like this, because the perceived value of the MP3 player is high. All you have to do is integrate the promotion of the contest with your site. Plaster announcements of the contest and why you are having it on your home page and pump it at gigs.

Games are another way to break the ice with fans and bring audience participation into your set. A punk band that I was checking out had an "animal noise" contest halfway through their show. They picked three contestants and asked them to do their best imitation of any animal. The audience picked the best and the winner got a CD.

Web Sticker makes custom stickers, decals, bumper stickers, and labels for the purpose of advertising web sites. They have multiple uses and are a great promotional tool. These are also a great "free gift" for when somebody purchases your CD or other merchandise from your site, and can be handed out at concerts. Visit **http://www.websticker.com** for more info.

WebCards prints full color post cards with your web site printed on them. They are inexpensive and can be given away or mailed in order to promote your site. Postcards are perfect for announcing your arrival on the web to existing fans. You could also use them to announce any new releases or events. Visit **http://www.webcards.com** for more info.

Prime Linx Inc. sells chrome plates to be placed on the back of your car with your web address. This would be a "subtle" way of announcing your arrival at gigs, while unloading gear, or on the road during tours. Only consider using this service if you have a short and memorable virtual domain name – i.e. http://www.yourbandname.com. It would look really silly if you had a long non-virtual domain name, like http://www.hubbagubbaisp.com/yourbandname. Visit **http://www.primelinx.com** for more info.

A Real Life Lesson in Killing Your Career

There are many other forms of publicity that musicians avoid because they think that being under budgeted prevents them access. When your press kit is ready to roll online, all you have to do is get it in front of the right eyes and let it do its job. The next chapter, *Using the Press to Your Advantage*, shows how to get more exposure from next to nothing, to spending a pile of money. Meanwhile, here is an entertaining short story with a valuable lesson in promotion...

I met a new client one night outside of a well-known record store. They were a Gangster Rap trio out of East Palo Alto and were very aggressive self-promoters. Needless to say, I was impressed by their unique method of "Direct Marketing." Here is how it worked.

In order to sell as many CD's as possible, they sat on the cars of customers and waited for them to come out of the record store. When the customer arrived at their vehicle one of the squatters would ask, "Did you find what you were looking for?", and, "What kind of music do you like?" No matter what the driver answered they would say, "Oh, we sampled some of that in our latest album. There is a little bit of everything in it for *everyone*." Then, like some super hero with a utility belt, the leader whipped out a CD and announced his band name and introduced the band members. "Our album is going to be in stores next month and we're in a bit of a hurry to get the word out. So we're selling our records at a reduced price - $4 for CD's and $2 for tapes...interested?" "Where else can you get a CD for $4 directly from an artist," I thought. I was impressed by their aggressiveness and since they were sitting on my car, I bought their CD and tossed my card at them.

After talking for a bit, I mentioned that I designed web pages for artists and do promotion too. They were so excited that they met with me again to hook me up with their artwork and bio. At that time I was mobile and did all my writing and design on the road with a laptop. When their site was finished, I downloaded it to my portable office and met them at a famous cafe in San Jose. I loaded their page right in front of them and showed how it worked - audio, links, and email - the whole bit from a tiny coffee stained monitor for the whole place to see. More than satisfied with my work, they paid their bill on the spot and wanted to talk more about their plans for an online attack. After we were done, they all got up and started to leave when a curious patron turned and asked one of the trio, "Hey, what were you guys doing on that laptop over there?" Everyone in the cafe stopped silent and turned towards him for the answer, "Ah, nothin'...we just got our web site designed." He turned and walked out the door. In a panic I yelled, "Yeah...and it's at www.<kept-a-secret-to-protect-the-innocent>.com!!!"

The End

Lesson: The trio had the perfect opportunity to whip out more CD's and mention their web site with the full attention of an audience. Instead, they proceeded to another record store to squat on more cars. Some habits never die.

Unfortunately, they made a distinction between their offline and online presence. This was a mistake that cost them. Not only did their web site fail, so did their sales. They were so intent on getting the word out through "direct marketing," they neglected press coverage and online promotion. So the moral of the story is that promoting your web site is just as important online as it is offline. Even though the means are different, the end result is the same. Don't ever pass up the opportunity to mention your web site or pass out business cards imprinted with it. *By the way, what the heroes of our story did to sell records can be considered as loitering and harassment. 'nuf said.*

TIME TO CHECK IN:

• **Raise Awareness Offline**

❑ Join An Organization

A great way to meet new people and gain more resources. There are also online organizations to join. You have no excuses to avoid networking! See *Networking* to find out where you can meet more people online and offline.

❑ Send Press Kit and Releases

Start with the local press and balloon out statewide and then regionally and eventually nationally. See next chapter on how to create appealing press releases.

❑ Update Literature & Merchandise

Everything you own should have your web address on it.

❑ Alternate Forms of Promotion

Stickers, Posters, Postcards are more affordable that you think!

NOTES:

NOTES:

CHAPTER 6

Using the Press to Your Advantage

With a web-based press kit, publicity has never been easier to achieve. The most common forms of publicity come from local newspapers, radio, trade publications and on-line ezines - electronic magazines. Because publicity is free, the greatest challenge is in getting editors to publish or broadcast your material. Regardless of what part of the music business you are in, you should look for as much publicity as possible. A well-planned publicity effort will yield maximum results: free advertising that raises awareness and confirmation of your talents. This chapter talks specifically about what a press release should look like and how to submit materials to traditional print media, as well as online media.

Writing Successful Press Releases

A press release tells a story about you and your music or an event that has recently occurred or is about to happen. It has a distinct format that journalists and editors recognize: headline, body, and conclusion. There are several other formats, but this is the most widely used. See *Anatomy of a Press Release* on the next page. However, following this format does not guarantee that it will be published. Let's take a look at what you can do to create a successful press release:

- *Use a catchy HEADLINE:*
  Make your audience curious with a short, catchy headline. Remember, editors are looking for something that will make the content of their publications sizzle.

- *Provide facts in the BODY:*
  Once the reader has moved past the headline provide them with a brief description of the news worthy item, followed by facts and quotes from credible sources that validate your claim.

- *FORMAT your press release correctly:*
  A press release should be formatted according to well known guidelines. Otherwise it will get tossed into the circular filing cabinet.

- *Issue your press release with TIMELINESS:*
  Monday through Thursday is when most reporters look for stories. Call ahead if you are not sure. Also, submit your materials at least *ten business days* in advance. This is will give you a huge edge!

- *CONTACT / BOOKING INFORMATION:*
  Include all of your contact information: your name or agent, artist or band name, address, phone, fax, email, and web address. Be sure to end your press release with a single line containing three pound signs: **###**

Anatomy of a Press Release

- Use a catchy HEADLINE
  Create intrigue to grab attention
  Keep it short and concise.
  Limit your headline to one targeted sentence
- Provide facts in the BODY
  Introduction: A brief description of your news worthy music.
  Body: Details and explanation of your music with facts and quotations to build credibility.
  Conclusion: Include contact information and if possible, information about your publisher or distributor.
- Limit the press release to a max of 350 words
- End the release with 3 pound signs: ###

Cover Me - I'm Going In...

A cover letter should be addressed to the person you want to consider your material. Focus on a brief personal note. It should be typed and tell the recipient that the attached material is new and of interest to his/her audience. With email and fax technology, it is easy to forget this important element in the presentation.

When to Issue a Press Release

It is only appropriate to issue a press release when your group:

- Launches a new album.
- Has won a prestigious award.
- Is playing at a community event or involved in other special events.
- Enters into a record deal or is acquired by a new distributor.

However, keep in mind the audience of the publication receiving your release. Are they local? National? International? A nationally distributed publication would most likely not consider your performance at a community event newsworthy, unless it is aligned with their interests. Also, local publications would be the only ones interested in announcing that your group is available to play weddings.

Who Cares?!

In addition to general music publications and media, choose mediums that are most likely to review your material. If you write jazz, try to find specific publications that carry similar write-ups on a regular basis. Always include a cover letter addressed to the contact person. If no one is publishing your releases or you are not getting results, your release is most likely not newsworthy. Rewrite it and try again.

Biography vs. Press Release

A bio tells the whole story of the artist, influences and where the group is headed. Make sure your bio tells a good story - something with metaphor or describing your work with "colors." Whatever you do, don't include in your bio about learning an instrument "early in life." Answer the question of what makes you different. Don't forget your cover letter and catchy headline! With all of this in mind, let's explore the psychology of an editor.

Understanding An Editor's Needs

Press releases must be developed carefully and the proper format followed. That means your release must sell the editor by first and foremost being "newsworthy." Remember that editors receiving your material are aware of your intent - free advertising. Their job is to provide useful information to readers.

Additionally, editors have little time to examine your material. A well-written release saves them time and effort. You must design your release to appeal to an editor's personal needs, i.e. how your material will benefit their readers or listeners. Leave out the guesswork by providing the most information possible in a compact space. If an editor is hungry for more, you will be contacted or possibly interviewed.

How to Turn the Other Cheek

If your first attempt fails to generate publicity, try rewriting from a different angle. Make sure you are sending it to the proper contact and try again. Remember, a release has to stand out yet fit with the information that editors provide in their publication. With newspapers, gauge your material to be in the hands of the editor in time for the Sunday edition. There is generally more space available then. Be sure to call ahead for the deadline.

Do's and Don'ts

Your efforts will fail if you send material to the advertising, circulation, or business managers stating that you are an industry heavy or by placing short time constraints. They don't care because they are doing you a favor. Instead, make contact with the sole person who has the final say on publishing or

---

Press Release Layout

For Immediate Release

Date:
Subject of Interest: Music Business Daily

Your Name:
Band / Act:
Contact Info:

CATCHY HEADLINE

PROVIDE FACTS IN THE BODY

CONTACT INFORMATION

- ### -

broadcasting your material. Find out their name and a little about them and try to gain direct contact with them.

When your material is released, *always* send a short thank you note. Never call and demand to know why your material wasn't used, your words were changed, or only short mention was given. The editor who did you a favor will throw away your next release unopened.

Media Resources Available for National Exposure

Still hungry for national exposure? It *is* within your grasp! All it takes is a coordinated press release campaign. If you have a budget, there is an excellent online service that can write and/or distribute a targeted press release overnight: The News Bureau at **http://www.newsbureau.com**. You can target music related publications for as little as $125.

> Even though national exposure is possible, it is always better to focus locally where people can come and see you!

How about a free service to announce an event? Visit **http://www.businessnewswire.com** to submit your name and number. This is an awesome way to let the world know you are sponsoring an event, giving away free stuff, having a contest, holding a chat, or launching a "new and unique" Internet experience from your web site.

How do you find decent publications? You can narrow down your initial search by visiting indie resource sites like Band Utopia, Indie Music, and IndiePromo.com. Each have searchable databases with nothing but music industry publications. Band Utopia can be found at **http://www.bandutopia.com**, Indie Music is located at **http://www.indie-music.com**, and IndiePromo.com has its database at **http://IndiePromo.com/ezines**. However, the quality of some of the publications in these resources is left up to your determination.

If you want to build your own quality media contacts, there is an online database called MediaFinder: **http://www.mediafinder.com**. You can do a simple search by category for free. For a small fee, you can do more complex searches to find more relevant contacts in your market – i.e. Punk publications, etc. The publications listed in this resource are professional.

There is also a handy press release utility called, MediaMagnet that automates sending your press releases to related publications from your computer. You can download it and send to five media resources free or pay the $20 monthly subscription to enable the 10,000 plus media contacts - a real bargain if you promote for several groups or run a label. This utility also lets you put in your own media contacts into a common database. Visit: **http://www.mediamagnetpro.com** to get your hands on this useful program.

For the less web savvy, visit your local library. It has a wonderful collection of directories that contain every address and phone number for every type of media in the United States. These directories list newspapers, magazines, radio stations, and television companies - broadcast and cable. The most comprehensive directory is the *Gale Directory of Publishing and Media*. This vast resource is used by all of the major public relation firms and advertising agencies. Just visit any library and ask where you can get your hands on one. They are organized by state and then by city.

Online Resources for Offline Publications

Band Utopia
http://www.bandutopia.com

Indie Music
http://www.indie-music.com

IndiePromo.com
http://IndiePromo.com/ezines

MediaFinder
http://www.mediafinder.com

Media Magnet
http://www.mediamagnetpro.com

Tracking Your Success

How do you know if your issued press releases have generated coverage? Well, there are "clipping services" available to watch targeted publications for a fee. You can also use search engines and various other free services online to check newsgroups, mailing lists and key web sites. Keep an eye on your site, too. Main feedback can come in many forms including inquiries to the contact person mentioned in the press release, additional traffic to the web address published in your release, and increased sales action or inquiries. Remember that the same press release may yield completely different results in different publications and seasons. It's all about timing, so don't be discouraged. *Measuring Your Success* helps you analyze your results in more detail.

TIME TO CHECK IN:

- ## Draft Press Release In Established Format

  ❑ Catchy Headline
    Pique your audience's interest with a short catchy headline.

  ❑ Provide Facts in the Body
    Give a brief description of your news worthy item and then back it up with facts.

  ❑ Contact / Booking Information
    This is the perfect opportunity to take advantage of free advertising for your web site.

  ❑ End the Release with 3 Pound Signs: ###
    This signifies THE END!

- ## Draft A Cover Letter

  ❑ Get the Name of the Contact
    Contact the media you are interested in submitting your material to and get a contact name. Important!

  ❑ Customize Your Letter For Each Contact
    Do not address your letters "To Whom It May Concern". Use the name of the individual that has final say in releasing your material

  ❑ Include Your Events Calendar
    If the publication is in your local area or has a representative nearby, they may send somebody over to your show to observe your talent for later review in their publication.

- ## Draft A Biography

  ❑ A Bio Can Be Used Instead of a Press Release
    A bio can be used when nothing new is happening with your music, but you still want to get the word out.

• Gather More Media Contacts

❏ **Find Ezines That Cover Your Genre of Music**
Between MediaFinder, Band Utopia, Indie Music, and IndiePromo.com you will cover a lot of online and offline territory. They all have online searchable databases for offline publications.

❏ **Fanzine or Music Scene Rags**
No matter where you live there are always local music scene publications! When you tour, find publications that cover the area you will be gigging in and send your press materials.

❏ **Gale Directory of Publishing & Media**
Visit your local library and do some research. You can find TV and Radio Stations, magazines, and newspapers. This is only a last resort.

NOTES:

NOTES:

CHAPTER 7

Using Email Effectively

Email is an incredible tool. With it, you can keep fans informed of your progress, announce new music and gigs, contact the press, collect input, join discussion groups, etc. However at the same time, you could very easily cause damage to your online presence by abusing it. In this chapter, we will explore both the good and bad of email.

Besides growing awareness of your music and selling albums, a web site's function is to generate as many email contacts as possible. Realistically, well over eighty-percent of visitors will not make themselves known to you. Even when your site's traffic is steady, few visitors will still take the time to send you an email. This is not unusual, so don't be discouraged. However, if you find that every visitor that comes through your site is not making contact, then you need to seriously reassess your web site's effectiveness. In the meantime, let's start with the basics.

Building a Mailing List - Death of a Salesman

Building a list of contacts is key to online promotion. It is not enough to place an email or "contact" link on your site. Visitors are always in a hurry and even though they may be interested in your music, they are more likely to just pass on by. In this section, we are going to cover the different ways to encourage surfers to give you their email address.

There isn't any technology that allows you to capture visitors' email addresses without their knowledge or consent. The next best way is to make contacting you as effortless as possible. So how do you make surfers "click happy?" The following tips will help:

- **Keep Your Email Link in Plain View.** Make sure that your email address is visible on the front page of your site and a link is on every other page to all of your contact information. Whether it's new fans, first time visitors to your site, or A&R reps, all of them are frustrated by artists' web sites where they can't find a way to make contact.

The Easiet Way to Collect Email Addresses from Fans on
Your Site

```
<FORM METHOD="post"
ACTION="mailto:info@domain.com?subject=Send Info">
<INPUT TYPE="submit" VALUE="Click Me!"> </FORM>
```

The above code generates the button below - Click Me! - and sends an email to info@domain.com with the subject *Send Info*. This gimmick works by creating the path of least resistance. NOTE: the browser transmitting must be configured with a name and email address.

Click Me!

- **Try Different Methods of Collecting Email Addresses.** Besides putting your email address in plain view as a link, you can use different ways to gather visitors' email addresses. One way is to place a button that generates an email message with one click. (See table with Single Button Click example above.) Another way is to encourage people to sign your guest book. This way you will not only get an email address, but a name and geographical location. There is also the classic text field and "submit button," which takes a bit of web programming knowhow. Combining these different methods will constantly encourage visitors to give you their email address.

- **Encourage Visitors to Comment on Your Music/Site.** If your site has a lot of "wow" factor and interactivity, you could really clean up by asking visitors for input on your site or music. You could get some extremely valuable input on your site's effectiveness here, at the same time of accomplishing your goal of getting their email address.

- **Be a Giver, Not a Taker.** Give away free tickets or sponsor a contest with your album or merchandise as the prize. People love getting stuff for free, no matter how trivial. This is an effective way to encourage surfers to relinquish an email address. Other methods include holding a yes/no survey, requesting input, or having fans vote for their favorite song.

- **Confidentiality Is Your Responsibility.** Make clear your intentions to remove any doubt in visitors giving you their email address. A simple disclaimer will help: *Click here to win a free CD. Your address will be kept strictly confidential.* Web weary visitors want to stay in control. So be sure to give an option to unsubscribe from your mail list, as well. Likewise, you must not abuse your fans' trust in giving you their email address. Do not trade, sell, or give away your list, even to other artists. However, if you want to cross promote a gig with another band, draft up a common announcement and have every group involved, mail it to their lists themselves. When you give something hard-earned away, others tend to take it for granted and use it incorrectly. By doing this, you protect yourself from other groups abusing your list. I'm not saying don't share your list, just stay in control of it.

How to Effectively Use Email

A major function of a web site is to encourage surfers to make personal contact through email. When a visitor does make contact, your web site has done its job and generated a contact. So what do you do now? *Promote yourself through customer service.* How you handle a new contact is essential to generating word-of-mouth buzz and closing CD sales quickly. Remember that every email you send is a representation of you and each recipient is a potential customer. The following five tips will show that you mean business:

Email Do's

- **Be Prompt and Professional:** Check your email regularly and respond promptly to any inquiries. When you become too busy to respond, the time has come to hire somebody to handle your PR! Keep in mind, there is no such thing as firing off a *quick* reply. Spend some time creating form letters - thank you, introduction, and announcement letters. Avoid slang and double check your spelling.

- **Messages in Plain Text:** It is important that your message get across clearly. In the past, different desktop computers could not communicate or pass data to one another because of dissimilar formats. Fortunately, the Internet has helped a great deal in closing the gap between PC's, Mac's, and other operating systems. Still, each has its own way of formatting messages and can result in extra "garbage" characters in a recipient's mailbox. For example, many email programs and web browsers can send email in HTML, delivering garbage to recipients with incompatible email readers. Before firing off anything, make sure that your email software is configured to send "plain text" only - not MIME, Rich Text, HTML, etc.

If you have the knowhow, you can add an option for subscribers to choose between HTML or plain text formats. Of course, you will have to maintain two separate lists and distribute your newsletter in two different formats. This can be a great deal of work for a small group. Unless your mail list is large, it may not be worth your time to pursue this course of action.

- **Email Signatures:** A good businessperson never conducts correspondence without including basic contact information. The same applies to email. Most email programs can automatically append an electronic "letterhead" with basic contact information known as a **signature** or **sigfile**. Some email programs also double as a newsgroup browser, allowing your signature to be added to posts as well. An effective signature should be no more than four lines:

  - Headline / Short Blurb / Tag
  - Email Address
  - Web Address

How to Create an Effective Email Signature

Before you get too excited about creating an email signature, think very carefully about the headline item. It shouldn't describe you or your music. (Yes, I said <u>should not</u>.) Instead, a headline should describe your web site. The point of a signature is to create interest. This can be done with a headline that is either intriguing or blunt. For example, an intriguing headline would be akin to, "What are Lullabies for Fatigued Metal?"; a blunt headline, "Get your free CD of the Ralph Mongers."

Often times, the name of a band says it all. Concentrate on how to make people regret never having visited your web address. Plus, most popular email programs will make the email and web address in your signature, a link within the message itself. This makes it all the easier for curious readers of your headline to click on impulse. Now that's dangerous advertising!

```
┌─────────────────────────────────────────────────┐
│                                                 │
│              Example Signature                  │
│                                                 │
│  --                                             │
│                                                 │
│  ─────────────────────────────────────────      │
│  What are Lullabies for Fatigued Metal?         │
│  Visit http://www.filmscoring.com/ to find out more │
│  mailto:info@filmscoring.com                    │
│                                                 │
└─────────────────────────────────────────────────┘
```

Notice the example above doesn't include a phone number or physical address. You certainly don't want phone calls from Cambodia at 2am on Sunday mornings, and wouldn't want 4 billion complete strangers to know where you live. With a post office box and voice mail, you can shield yourself from any online *weirdness* if you choose to publish your offline contact information.

Some Simple Sig Hints

• The first line consists of two dashes and a space - at the far left. This signals email programs to remove the signature in replies.

• A signature should not exceed four lines.

• Place *http://* in front of the URL. Most email programs translate this into a clickable link within the message.

• Place *mailto:* in front of the email address to create a reply link within the message!

Email Don'ts:

• **Unsolicited Attachments:** Most email programs allow you to include files in a message. Some artists have abused this function by mass mailing an attached audio file and/or picture to A&R reps, fans, etc. This is an action that will earn you the title of *Spammer*. Be sure you have a recipient's permission before sending any attachments. "Why", you ask? Attachments increase the size of your message by a great deal and can lock out its recipients from receiving any further email! This is because a size limit may be placed by the receiving ISP. In fact, some companies and ISPs ignore attachments, entirely! Furthermore, attachments add unnecessary upload time to your message and download time for the recipient. If you want to distribute a song, put it on the web and email its URL. A carefully written email announcement will pique enough interest and avoid angering your online audience.

- **That Bcc Thingie:** Don't you hate it when an email contains every single recipient in the message. This is the email you get when it takes scrolling past five screenfulls of email addresses before seeing one measly sentence, announcing a concert that happened two nights ago. This does nothing more than anger recipients, encourage spamming, compromise the confidentiality of fan's email addresses, and show that the sender is an amateur. Typically, someone in the recipient list decides to "reply all" and either complain, unsubscribe, or send out an unrelated announcement in retaliation. The solution is simple! Every email program comes with what is commonly called a Blind Courtesy Copy or Blind Carbon Copy (bcc:) feature. Blind copying (a.k.a. bcc'ing) allows mass mailing without revealing the entire list to each recipient. See your email program's help section for more information. Bcc is not always in plain view, so you may have to dig around a bit. Newbie-U's web site has an email program tutorial that covers this, as well. Visit their site to find out more: http://www.newbie-u.com/email.

Spam! Spam! Spam!

Online privacy is one of the hottest topics debated since the opening of the *Wild Wild Web*. Spam is at the center of it all. Spam is an Internet term that originated from the newsgroup community describing overzealous posters. It has since been adopted by users of email. Spam also refers to unsolicited messages sent to individual email addresses repeatedly to a mass number of users online. It's the junk mail of the new millennium. Many, if not all, Spam messages are commercial or self-promoting. They are unwanted by everyone.

How to Destroy Your Career Overnight

What Spammers fail to realize is that they waste the time and money of millions of people. Spammers make online users wade through a pile of junk email before getting to their regular email. If Spam is not discouraged by users and system administrators, alike, the Internet would be in danger of coming to a screeching halt.

If It's So Bad Then Why Do They Do It?

It's cheap. With any email account, a Spammer can send messages to hundreds, thousands, even millions of email addresses at the click of a button. A Spammer only needs to send a single email one time, to reach a large number of people, whereas a phone call, fax, or letter would take days and many hours of manpower to send out.

So Where Do I Draw The Line?

A simple answer is, if you are sending email to people you don't know or to addresses that you have gotten through "questionable means," i.e. stealing or slurping from message boards then **you are spamming**. Even the most innocent announcement to unsuspecting recipients can be considered Spam. When I first started out, I sent out announcements for an online chat about "online promotion" to a list of emails I misappropriated from a popular message board. For all of my trouble I found that almost half of the addresses where "dead" and the rest complained about my invasion of their privacy. Luckily the Web Master of that message board was kind enough to let me off with a warning and didn't slander my name online. Lesson learned...I tell you this only to spare you of any future humiliation.

- **Generate Initial Traffic To Your Site Through Email**

  ❏ Create A Signature File

     With a signature file configured in your email and newsgroup programs every post and email you send will have your essential contact information - email, URL, and Band Name. You can go as far as to place a couple of your upcoming shows into your signature file.

  ❏ Draft Your "Arrival on the Web" Announcement for Existing Fans

     Keep it short and to the point. Word it so that visitors will know why they should visit your site. Just try to pique interest; don't give the hard sell. Try offering something free or have a contest of some sort.

  ❏ Email Existing Fanbase

     If you don't have any email addresses of your fans, start collecting them at concerts. If you don't gig…start gearing up for the rest of your promotion campaign.

  ❏ Grow Your Own Email List

     Try to make giving an email address the easiest and quickest thing visitors can do on your site. By doing this early on, you are preparing your site for the new fans arriving at your site, generated by your promotion efforts.

NOTES:

NOTES:

Reality Check: Integrating Your Online Promotion with Offline Efforts

Even though we have said this before, it bears repeating before we move into the next section.

Many artists make the mistake of thinking that all they need to do is get their music online and they will be discovered. Don't fall into this trap yourself. All of your marketing efforts should be coordinated to work online and offline. By doing this you will generate more visitors and leverage more publicity. The Internet is not a departure from the traditional methods of promotion. However, as technology improves, this situation could change over time.

SECTION III

Promoting Your Web Site Online

CHAPTER 8

Understanding Search Engines

Search engines are huge online directories of web sites that surfers use to find a topic of interest. Search engines also help to create some order out of the chaos on the Internet. Although search engines only index a small portion of the Internet, they are still vast resources with content on any subject imaginable. How your site stands out among the masses is the real task at hand. The key in successfully using search engines is knowing how each type works. In this chapter, we are going to explore the three basic and most important types of search engines: Deep, Directories and Human Driven.

Using Search Engines to Gain Exposure

Having a web site on the Internet is not enough. You need to "file" or register your site with the various search engines. Surfers won't know where to find you without these handy online directories. With some carefully selected keywords and page titles, surf weary visitors will more likely find your site among the vast sea of web pages.

The top six search engines each receive tens-of-thousands of add requests per day and growing. They are AltaVista, Excite, HotBot, InfoSeek, Lycos, and Yahoo. See the table on this page for their web addresses.

In light of this, the layout and design of a Web site is more important than ever. A new trend has emerged where search engines are censoring second rate web pages from users. Although search engines may seem overloaded, don't ignore them as a potential resource for visitors. When a Web page starts to gain popularity, fans will link it to theirs and those links will be found in search engines as well. The more your site appears on a search engine the higher the ranking. This phenomenon is known as *link popularity* and some search engines use this to help determine a site's importance.

The Big 6
AltaVista
www.altavista.com
Lycos
www.lycos.com
Infoseek
www.infoseek.com
Excite
www.excite.com
Yahoo
www.yahoo.com
HotBot
www.hotbot.com

The Three Basic Search Engines

Deep Search Engines - Spiders & Robots

Deep Search Engines are the most widely used and exist in greater numbers than Directories and Human Driven Engines. This makes Deep Engines the most important to get your site listed in. However, they are the trickiest to get good placement in and require careful preparation.

Deep Engines use a program called a *spider* or *robot* to decide your web page's main purpose. These autonomous "creatures" constantly roam the World Wide Web cataloging every new or updated page they find. When a spider visits a site, it compiles all of the sub-pages and then visits all links external to the site. If your site is not *linked* from another web site, it will never be found by a spider. Therefore, it is necessary to add yourself to a spider's search list. By submitting to Deep Search Engines, you are requesting that a spider visit your site as soon as possible, instead of waiting for it to find your site by chance among a vast sea of web sites.

> NOTE: Not every web designer will optimize a Web site for search engine submission. Even the most popular submission services - Submit-It! and Register-It! - will not optimize your page for you and they are typically used by said web designers. Ask if your designer includes keyword and title optimization. Otherwise you could be wasting time and money on a service that will get your site the lowest ranking possible... guaranteed.

Even though Deep Engines have strict requirements, they are the easiest to submit to. They only ask for the **URL** – web address - of your site and an **email** address. It can take up to eight weeks or as little as twenty-four hours before your site is listed. For a better listing within a Deep Search Engine you should carefully consider some appropriate keywords for your pages and their titles. The sections on *Improving Your Rankings* and *Preparing for Submission* cover this in great detail. Examples of search engines that use spiders are: **Infoseek, Excite, Lycos, Altavista, AOL Netfind, Northern Light and WebCrawler**. Except for Excite, all of these search engines make use of keywords for ranking.

Human Driven Search Engines

These search engines were created out of an effort to reduce cluttered listings and offer higher quality information for surfers. As a result, these engines are the most difficult to get into. This is because a flesh-and-blood human being makes the decision of whether or not to admit your site into their listings. They will also rank your site. So even if you get into these highly coveted search engines, you may get a low ranking, especially if your site falls short on presentation or quality of content. **About.com, Open Directory, and Yahoo!** are the most well known Human Driven search engines.

Every Human Driven search engine has unique submission qualifications. Visit each one and read carefully their requirements. Follow their instructions to the letter. Anything that will get in the way of your site being added, will. I recommend that you wait until your site gains somewhat of a reputation online before attempting entry into these highly exclusive search engines. This will give you an opportunity to perfect your site and fine tune your online presence before taking on the "big guns."

> ### The "Big" Human Driven Search Engines
>
> **About.com**
> http://www.about.com
>
> **The Open Directory**
> http://www.dmoz.org
>
> **Yahoo!**
> http://www.yahoo.com

Subject Specific Directories – or Just "Directories"

Unlike a true search engine, Subject Specific Directories contain lists of resources on a single subject, entered by users of the directory. These useful web sites usually have informative articles, classified ads, newsgroups, and message boards. Add yourself to every applicable directory you can find. They provide great targeted advertising for sites on specific topics. **IndiePromo.com**, for example, is a subject specific directory on indie promotion resources.

Preparing Your Site For Submission To The Various Search Engines

Now that you know the three major types of search engines, let's prepare your site for submission. Each type of engine has unique requirements that have to be integrated into your site. Deep Search Engines rely on keywords embedded into your web pages for cataloging; Human Driven Engines are maintained by hired professionals, and Directories are handled by you, the submitter. To help your overall search engine needs, we first need to consider which keywords are appropriate and how to put them into your web pages. This will drive the rest of the submission process.

How to Use Keywords To Improve Your Ranking in Deep Engines

You can improve your web site's search engine ranking by inserting a list of carefully selected keywords into the <META> tag of your HTML documents. If you don't know what a <META> tag is, don't worry. Most HTML editors will handle this for you. Look in your editor's documentation for "adding keywords" to your web pages. There are also completed examples throughout this chapter for your review. If you are a DIY'er and want to learn HTML programming, there is very useful free resource online just for you: **http://www.webreference.com**.

Before submitting a site to any search engine, read the next section carefully. This is the most crucial part of promoting your web site with search engines. If you choose keywords poorly, no amount of submissions or HTML tweaking will bring a highly targeted audience to your site.

Building A List of Targeted Keywords

Search engines determine how to categorize and rank your site *after* analyzing a web page's list of keywords. By inserting this information into your web pages, surfers will be to able find your site by entering any one of your relevant keywords into a search engine.

We will discuss how to place these important keywords into your HTML code, but first, let's create a list worthy for any search engine. Begin by writing down a short list of keywords and phrases that embody your musical style, abilities, name, the instruments you play, and your influences. Then rearrange them in order of importance.

An Excerpt From A Web Page with META Tags Prepared For Deep Engine Submission

```
<HEAD>
...
<META NAME="KeyWords" CONTENT="singer,lyricist,piano,rock">
...
</HEAD>
```

TIP: Place unique keyowrds in each web page. This will increase your diversity in Search Engines.

For example, if you want to be found on search engines as a singer and songwriter, arrange your list accordingly: "singer,song writer,songwriter,poet,vocalist,*name-or-band*,*your-influences*,rock,guitar,music." Notice that there are no spaces between commas, except in *song writer*. This is because many people spell it that way - right or wrong - and is called a *keyword phrase*.

Can't Think of Any Keywords?

A list of the most common keywords inputted on Yahoo! can be extremely valuable in picking the right keywords for your site. You can easily find a current list of most used web search terms at: **http://www.searchterms.com**. Check your list against theirs and see if there are more useful ones, as well. By the way, a great deal of the top 200 keywords entered into search engines are sexually explicit. Avoid the trap of putting some of these words into your keyword list. The aim is to focus your promotion on a tightly focused audience. Misleading people will not benefit your music or get you new fans.

Test Your Keywords

With your new list handy, visit the major search engines and enter each keyword one by one to see what a search will yield. Visit a few of the top listings and view the HTML source code. It can't hurt to take a peak at what your competition is doing! You may find more keywords in their <META> tags that you haven't thought of. This is a common practice in the "ranking war." High ranking sites get a lot of hits and may contain a keyword that is appropriate to your site.

Avoid pasting the entire string of <META> tags from top listings straight into yours. This is a bad idea and actually does little to improve your ranking. *You want your site to stand out from the rest. The only way to accomplish this is to customize your keyword list to the narrowest target audience possible.* Also, some keywords may be the intellectual property of the site that "inspired" your keywords. That means that you could potentially be sued for using a keyword in their list. A former Playboy Playmate was sued by the magazine for using "Playboy" in her keyword list.

Making Adjustments to Improve Your Rankings

Here are a couple things you can do to improve your placement:

- **Keywords Phrases:** With countless web sites on the Internet, surfers have learned to narrow down their searches by using *strings* of at least two or

```
+----------------------------------------------------------------------+
|                    Completed META Tag Example                        |
|                                                                      |
| <HEAD>                                                               |
|    <TITLE>Ralph Mongers: Conservative Punk Music for Moms</TITLE>    |
|    <META Name="description" Content="Trial CD Available">            |
|    <META Name="keywords" Content="punk,free MP3s,anarchy">           |
| </HEAD>                                                              |
+----------------------------------------------------------------------+
```

three related words, for example "song writer" or "film composer" or "punk mp3." If you have both keywords listed separately, you will be listed below other pages that group both words together.

- **Plurals:** Once you've completed your list, make each word plural. Many surfers search for the plural of a word - "singers" or "writers" or "punk mp3s." If your keywords are in the singular, your page will be bypassed because a search on "singers" does not match on the word "singer," whereas "singer" is considered part of "singers." Also notice the instance of the words *"song writer"* in the previous example. Keep any potential misspellings in mind when selecting your keywords!

Using Your New Developed List of Keywords to Build an Effective Web Page Title

Now that you have selected and prioritized your keywords, let's apply them to the three elements of HTML code that search engines and spiders look at: <TITLE>, <META>, and page content within the body - i.e. the pictures and links that surfers see. Again if you are not familiar with HTML code, most editors will take care of this for you. See your HTML editor's documentation.

<TITLE> Tags - It's All In the Name

The HTML <TITLE> tag is the caption that appears on the title bar of your browser and is the "clickable" link in search engine lists. It is by far the most valuable tag, yet most amateur web designers overlook this hidden resource. Spiders consider the <TITLE> of a page to be the description of its content and look at this tag first. They also check to see if any of a page's <META> keywords are in the <TITLE>, using some archaic algorithm. When a match occurs, a keyword is considered to have *high density* and is therefore an important word that describes a site's content. Pages that have high density keywords are ranked *above* other web pages that don't.

Thus, we have come to the point of this section. Mix your <TITLE> and keywords carefully. Use only a few of the most powerful words from your list. Avoid making your <TITLE> as long as the equator. Keep in mind a human is doing the "clicking" so a listing at position #1 containing only disjointed keywords might not generate as much traffic as a descriptive caption partially down the same list, at position #10. Unless your site consists of only one page, spread your wealth of keywords to the rest of your sub-page <TITLE>s. See the completed example on the previous page.

<META> Tags - Keywords and Descriptions

META keywords are important but they rank below <TITLE>s and page content in importance. This is a trade secret among established web masters. Some Deep Search Engines depend mainly on <META> tags - Alta Vista and Infoseek are prime examples. By placing keyword-rich <META> tags in each of your pages - home and sub-pages - you will diversify your entire web site within search engines when you submit each page on your site.

When a site is listed within a search engine query - a *hit* - the <TITLE> of each matching web page appears as the clickable link. Following each title is the <META Name="description"> segment which is the informative description the surfers will see. The <META Name="keywords"> is how most engines determine site content, along with <TITLE> and <BODY> keywords. With a good layout the first few lines of

---

How <META> Tags Appear In The <HEAD>
Segment of HTML Documents

```
<HEAD>
    <TITLE>Your Page Title Here: Some Top Keywords</TITLE>
    <META Name="description" Content="Your description here">
    <META Name="keywords" Content="Your keyword list here">
</HEAD>

<BODY> (use of keywords in headings and content) </BODY>
```

---

your web page content - `<BODY>` section - will contain the most important words of your keyword list. Again, most search engines consider `<TITLE>` more important than the `<META Name="keywords">` list. Therefore, place only a few of the most pertinent keywords in the `<TITLE>` tag. See the table on the previous page entitled, *How <META> Tags Appear In The <HEAD> Segment of HTML Documents.*

TAG TIPS

- Keep each `<META>` tag on a single line or they will get cut short. Otherwise, your keyword list won't be effective enough to reach your audience. Even worse, your description will be cut short and confuse search engine users.

- Do not repeat the same keyword more than 3 times - any more and the entire list is ignored or your page will get a low ranking - i.e. the bottom.

BAD:
singer, singer, singer, vocalist, vocalist, vocalist

BAD:
singer, vocalist, singer, vocalist, singer, vocalist

GOOD:
singer, vocalist

- Restrict META descriptions to 25 words or less (under 150 characters) - including spaces and commas. Otherwise some engines will cut it short. Staying within this limit will make your site compatible with every search engine it encounters.

- A META *description* does not need keywords, so make it eye catching like a newspaper headline. This is the text that convinces a surfer to click on your site title. It is there to provide search engines with an explanation of contents for potential visitors.

- A META description should describe your web site, not you. The trick is to get surfers to visit your site. Always tell them why they should or what will benefit them by doing so. A great incentive is to offer free stuff and music samples. Once a surfer arrives, the layout and page content will take care of the rest.

- To increase search engine diversity, write a different META description and <TITLE> for each sub-page, while keeping the same list of keywords reordered to match content.

- When a deep search engine visits a page it catalogs every word. It is important to have your chosen list of keywords within the first few lines of the content of your home page.

Keyword Density In Your Web Page Content

Another high density combination is possible between the <BODY> and <META> tags. As in the <TITLE>, deep search engines also rank pages by keyword density within a page's content. For example, if a page contained the words "rock music" in its content and <META> tag, then a search engine query for "rock music" would put that page at the top of the list because it has 100% density of the keywords searched. *It doesn't matter how many times a keyword appears in a document, only the ratio of keywords in a page to the words in a query.*

Advanced Tips

One of the slickest ways to get your name to appear more frequently in a search engine's database is to diversify your site. This is achieved by submitting every web page within your site as a unique URL. For example, you have a home page, bio page, and hopefully an audio samples page. Each may have the following URL:

> **Home Page URL:** http://www.yourbandname.com
> **Bio URL:** http://www.yourbandname.com/bio.html
> **Audio URL:** http://www.yourbandname.com/audio.html

At all of the major search engines, submit each of the above and any other relevant pages within your site. Make sure that each page contains a link to one another. Here is another trick - and guard this one well - submit any other page that makes mention of you: directories, link lists, ezines, and fan pages. Be sure to submit the exact URL that links to your site, not the root address - i.e. *http://www.yourfan.com/links/yadda.html*, not *http://www.yourfan.com*.

The more your site appears on other web pages the more diverse your site will be. This phenomenon is known as link popularity and is an important factor in getting a top listing within search engines. But before you dash off to every search engine, be sure to read *Submitting to Search Engines*, and *To Yahoo! Or Not To Yahoo!*

Picking Good Titles for Your Web Pages

Write a single natural sentence describing your site in the spirit of a newspaper head-line. This is the link that surfers will see in search engines when they get a "hit" on your page. By doing this, you not only help search engines categorize your site, but will make it more enticing for fans to visit. This is the most effective use of <TITLE> tags within your HTML code. Using our earlier site example:

Home Page Title:
Your Band Name: Music for the discerning Filmmaker.

Bio Page Title:
Your Band Name: Documentary of Film Composer John Dawes.

Audio Page Title:
Your Band Name: Free audio samples of Film Music. Order CD's

Writing Effective Web Page Descriptions for Search Engines

First and foremost, use the <META> Description tag to describe your site, not you. Write a two to three sentence description relevant to each page's content. Here is one for the Home Page:

Affordable music for TV, film, and multimedia. Free demonstra-tion CD available upon request. Visit today to hear free samples and see video clips.

This may not be a boost to my artistic integrity, but I have learned in of all my experi-ence that artistic integrity does not bring in work or sell records - good business sense does. (This explains why less deserving / talented artists get radio air play; their business sense is in sync with the public eye.) As soon as I finish recording music, I immediately switch into "business mode" and treat my CD as a product.

A web site should do the same in order to get the word out. The trick is to get someone to click-through to your site from a search engine. Once there, you can make your site's content reflect your artistic integrity or go for the hard sale. It is entirely up to you. Just do what ever it takes to get visitors into the door! As much as this may hurt, I always try to remember that I only spend ten-percent of my time creating music and the rest trying to get it in the hands of useful people. This is how your site will appear in search engines using the method above in *Picking a Good Title for Your Web Pages* and in this section:

> **John Dawes: Music for the discerning Filmmaker.**
> **Affordable music for TV, film, and multimedia. Free demonstration CD available upon request. Visit today to hear free samples and see video clips.**

The link "John Dawes: Music..." gives the hard sell and the description "Affordable..." follows through with benefits. You can't loose with this combo. To help you with more page title and description ideas, see the completed example for fictional singer/songwriter Angela Voce below, and the *Search Engine Result* at end of this chapter.

A Completed <TITLE> and <META> Tag Example For Fictitious Artist, Angela Voce:

```
<HEAD>
<TITLE>Angela Voce: Singer, Songwriter</TITLE>
<META Name="description"
Content="Home Page of vocalist Angela Voce - Listen to Music
- Win a FREE CD.">
<META Name="keywords"
Content="singers,vocalists,songwriters,song,writers,angela
voce,the three divas">
</HEAD>
```

It Bears Repeating Again!

ADVICE: Not every web designer will optimize a Web site's `<META>` and `<TITLE>` tags for search engine submission. Even the most popular submission services - Submit-It! and Register-It! - will not optimize your HTML code and they are used by said web designers. Ask if your web master includes search engine optimization in their web design package. Otherwise, you could be wasting time and money on a service that will get your site the lowest ranking possible...guaranteed.

High Rollers

The strength of a keyword diminishes in the main body of a page, the further down it is placed. Try to place plenty of keywords in the first few lines of text within the `<BODY>`. `<H1>` or `<H2>` heading tags at the top of a page are also helpful. Use these tags rather than font size to emphasize the importance of your headlines to search engines. HTML browsers automatically use a larger font size when text is encapsulated by `<H1></H1>` and `<H2></H2>`, etc. See Web Reference's HTML online tutorial for more information on do-it-yourself HTML programming - **http://www.webreference.com**.

The Alphabetical Issue

Deep search engines have never placed any significance on the alphabetical ranking of a page `<TITLE>`. The only real advantage with a low alphabetical title is if you have already made the grade into a Yahoo! category. Even though these categories have hundreds of listings, you will still stand out from the rest of the millions. Don't loose sleep on not calling your band, *AAA Punk.* However, with Directories, entries may be alphabetically listed. Be sure to check the subject you want to submit to and see if this is the case.

Trouble Spots to Avoid

Keyword Repetition

Until recently, crafty web masters could get away with listing keywords in `<!--` *comment tags* `-->` repetitively, but search engine administrators got wise to this and actively penalize this method - to the bottom you go.

Camouflaged Text

Another gimmick that will penalize your ranking is, placing your keyword list within your page content, especially if it is the same color as the background. One can still get around this by using a different tint, which still makes keywords invisible to the naked eye but visible to spiders. Infoseek has publicly declared that their spider ignores "camouflaged" pages.

Changing Titles

Regularly changing the title of a web page used to be an effective way to achieve diversity in deep engines. When a spider processed a site, it thought a new <TITLE> tag represented a new page and gave it a new listing. This is no longer the rule of thumb as spiders have become more sophisticated.

Online Tools To Help You Out

Before submitting URLs, you need to be ready for primetime. They should be perfect for both spiders and humans to process. Here are some tools to help you fine tune and measure the performance of your pages.

Web Site Garage is a free service that checks any URL pointed to it. The "garage" can check a page's load time, spelling, and HTML integrity. It also reports link popularity and any dead links. **Tagmaster** is another program that checks your <META> tags

---

Online Tools That Automate Enhancing Your Site

TagMaster
http://www.tagmaster.com

Web Monkey
http://www.webmonkey.com

Web Site Garage
http://www.websitegarage.com

---

and makes recommendations as well. See *Internet Resources* for more online tools to check your site's web pages.

Link Popularity

Alta Vista and Infoseek can tell you how many pages are linked to your site. All you have to do is put *link:* in front of your URL and do a search, like so: *link:http://www.domain.com.* This is a great way to do a quick check on your progress.

Search engine submission can be the most time consuming part of web site design. Most professional web designers have the software and knowledge to complete this task effortlessly. If you don't mind putting down more money on search engine submission software, we strongly recommend doing so. (Read the next chapter first!) Otherwise, ask your web designer if submission *and* keyword optimization is included in your package deal.

A Final Word

With enough powerful keywords and a few sub-pages, you can diversify your site on any search engine. Sub-pages are treated the same and they can benefit from the use of <TITLE> and <META> tags, as well. Take advantage of this. Each sub-page has more specific information than your home page and can also be tailored for higher keyword density. This will increase the odds of your site being seen near the top - perhaps with its sub-pages. With some creative writing in your page content - <BODY> segment - you can make use of a page's three most important keywords. Your site will then be ready for submission to every type of search engine on the Internet. After a few weeks of waiting for your submissions to be processed, you can concentrate on growing traffic through other online methods in conjunction with offline techniques.

TIME TO CHECK IN:

WARNING: Do not do any of the following until your web site is finished! Otherwise your search engine placement will be adversely affected. *Never* submit an incomplete site or one under construction!

- **Optimize Your Site For Every Search Engine: Deep, Directory, Human Driven**

  ❑ Select A List of Keywords
    Your keywords should embody your musical style, abilities, name, influences and the instruments you play.

  ❑ Prioritize Your Keywords
    Reorder your list based on how you want to market your abilities. Try to have unique keyword tags in every page.

  ❑ Make Your Keywords Plural
    Make each word in your list plural. Some surfers search on the plural of a word.

  ❑ Consider Misspellings
    If a word in your list is commonly misspelled, add it. For example "Web Design" is often misspelled as *"Web Desgin."*

  ❑ Test Your Keywords
    Visit all of the major search engines and perform a search on your top words. Visit the top listings and view their HTML code for the keywords that got them to the top. You may find more applicable words to your site. Don't paste or add their list into your HTML code. Be unique!

  ❑ Place Your Final Keyword Choices
    Put your keywords in order of importance on a single line in your HTML documents. All of the popular WYSIWYG web page editors take care of this for you.

  ❑ Write <META> Descriptions
    Write a different description for each page on your site. These are to be placed in the <META Name="description" Content="your description here!" > tag. Deep Search Engines use this tag to describe your page to visitors. WYSIWYG editors are helpful here, too.

❏ Use Top Keywords in <TITLE> tags

Write a unique title for each page on your site. These are to be placed between the <TITLE> & </TITLE> tags. Most search engines use this as the clickable link to your site. See example next page.

❏ Try To Use Top Keywords in <BODY>

Insert your most pertinent keywords into your page content. The heading tag enforces the importance of the words for some search engines - <H1> & </H1>, etc.

NOTE: http://www.webreference.com has a tutorial that can explain all of those <xxx> & </xxx> thingies. Since HTML programming is easily a subject for another book we recommend that you make use of their free tutorials.

The next page contains a sample search engine query on *taco truffles*. Two hits were generated. The first listing has the highest keyword density in the <TITLE> tag, earning it a top position. Its <HEAD> segment contains:

```
<TITLE>Taco Truffles</TITLE>
<META NAME="Description" CONTENT="Film Scoring for Hire">
<META NAME="KeyWords" CONTENT="film,music,movie,composer">
```

The <TITLE> and <META> *description* are used to describe the hits listed below. Notice no keywords are shown! These are internal to the Deep Search Engines. If the search had been done on *film music*, a different result would have emerged.

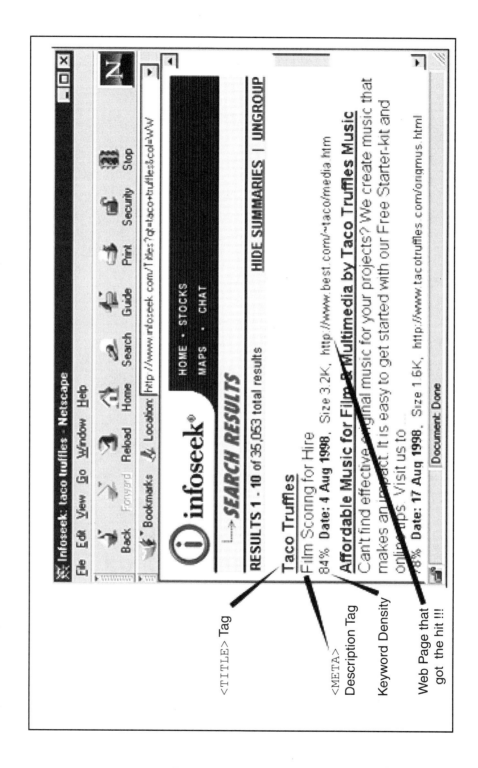

NOTES:

NOTES:

NOTES:

NOTES:

CHAPTER 9

Submitting to Search Engines

In the last chapter, we discussed how to integrate the requirements of the three types of search engines into your web pages: Deep, Directories, and Human Driven. In this chapter, we are going to explore how to submit to each type of these search engines, what to expect, and what to avoid.

Submitting To Deep Search Engines

Deep Search Engines should be your first stop because they are the easiest to submit to and cover the most "territory." The objective is to submit every page on your site that has a unique title and optimized keyword list, so that the right person will find the right page created for their needs – i.e. A&R Reps, fans, stray surfers, local press, etc. This will also ensure that Deep Engines will catalog your entire site and increase your diversity.

How to Submit

Deep Engines only ask for the **URL** - web address - of your site and an **email** address. Their spiders and robots will handle the rest while you wait to be listed. Only submit your home page, bio, music, press kit page, and any special event page. The key to getting a good listing in a Deep Search Engine is to avoid the following mistakes detailed below:

- **Only Submit When You Are Ready:** Double check your page titles and keyword lists to see if they target the audience you want to attract to your site. Begin submitting once they are in order, otherwise you may get a poor ranking. Make sure you have read and understand *Understanding Search Engines* before you begin.

- **Submission Limits:** Do not resubmit the same pages to search engines again and again to improve your rankings. Deep Engines only accept a limited number of URLs per domain. Many web masters become overzealous and try to submit to deep engines weekly. Avoid the temptation. Infoseek, for example, deals with repeated submission requests by removing all pages in their database for a whole domain. Ouch! Alta Vista only accepts ten URLs per domain per day, ignoring any further submissions.

- **Say "No Frames" Even When You Have Them:** Frames allow web masters to isolate areas on a web page with different content. A common use of frames is to have a menu on the left-hand side which remains static while the right-hand side's content is dynamic and can be scrolled up and down by visitors. Try to avoid using frames in your site's design. Search engines have difficulty with following links to sub-pages in other frames. If you already have them in your site's layout, use the <NOFRAMES> tag in your index or home page. This will help search engines deal with a framed site. You can find out more about frames and how to handle them at the Web Reference: *http://www.webreference.com*. There are a lot of excellent tutorials on many different aspects of web design there, and they are all free.

Submitting to Human Driven Search Engines

Human Driven Engines are the most difficult to get a listing in because flesh-and-blood human beings decide whether or not your site is worthy for their users. They each have different submission forms and unique requirements. The best way to get into Human Driven Engines is through "local" categories. For example, Yahoo! has a "get local" section that is well suited for band sites.

Also, the Open Directory and About.com have a section reserved just for bands. Your chance of getting into these two are greater than Yahoo!, especially if you are active and represent a particular genre well in your local area/press. Having your own virtual domain name will go a long way towards getting you into these exclusive search engines, as well. The next chapter, *To Yahoo! or Not To Yahoo!* covers how to effectively submit your site to the most popular of the Human Driven Search Engines.

> ## Human Driven Search Engines
>
> **About.com**
> http://www.about.com
>
> **The Open Directory**
> http://www.dmoz.org
>
> **Yahoo!**
> http://www.yahoo.com

Submitting To Standard Directories

Remember, Directories do not use spiders to catalog web pages. Instead, they are "maintained" by the submitters. In addition, each directory has a unique submission form that is usually detailed and lengthy. By having your pages optimized for Deep Search Engines, you can paste your optimized keyword list, description, and title into the submission form and handle the rest by hand.

There are countless numbers of Standard Directories and, no doubt, you will be spending hours surfing around finding the right categories in each one to place your URLs. With software - for a price – you can automate the submission process. However, new directories constantly pop-up and software manufactures have a hard time keeping up. The time and effort it takes to submit your site, even with software, is almost not worth the return in traffic. Plus, many of the sites that are submitted to with these "time saving" utilities are used by Spammers to get unsuspecting webmasters' email addresses. I recommend that you save Directories for when you have exhausted every other resource covered in this book.

What to Expect from the Major Search Engines

Even though we have covered the basics of search engines, understand that each one has their own nuance. In this section, we are going to explore what to expect from the majors so that you can easily monitor your progress. We will also help you avoid damaging any chance of getting listed appropriately within their ranks. In a blow-by-blow analysis, here they are:

Deep Engines:

AltaVista – **http://www.altavista.com:** typically adds a page within a few days. I've seen it fluctuate to as long as three weeks. With them, it is best to submit only a few pages at a time. To see which pages on your site are indexed, use the search phrase **url:yoursitename.com** (without http://)

Excite – **http://www.excite.com:** is the primary search engine for the AOL/ Netscape merger. A lot of surfers pass through there. Excite suggests that your submission will be added in about two weeks. Sometimes, it takes longer. Stay on top of them by watching your submission's progress. To do this, enter the search phrase **yoursitename.com**.

HotBot – http://www.hotbot.com: is another service that takes two weeks. The database underlying HotBot is also used by Yahoo!, Microsoft Network (MSN), and a number of other major search engines. The services that maintains the shared database, Intokomi, does not take submissions directly. For now, the best way to be included by the others is through HotBot. To track your site's progress, use the search phrase **domain:yoursitename.com**

Infoseek – http://www.infoseek.com: will take submissions in two ways: by their add URL form or by sending in a list of all the URLs on your site in an email to them. Infoseek is unpredictable. I've had no success measuring the time it takes to get listed. This is because they are usually backlogged with add requests. Infoseek will penalize you if you submit the same URL more than once per day by *never* indexing your site. In addition, you may find it difficult to get other pages on your site listed as well. For an update on progress, search on **url:yoursitename.com**

Lycos – http://www.lycos.com: has two databases. One uses the human driven Open Directory. In order to get into this database, you will have to do a search on your keywords to find out who is the watchdog for your category. I've had mixed results. If you plan out your site carefully and promote it diligently through the other means covered in this book, the watchdog may "discover" your site already and categorize it for you. To search on your site's progress, type in the URL(s) you submitted (with the http:// - i.e. http://www.musicpromotion.net/music/promotion). If you receive the cold and sterile "INTERNAL ERROR URL" message, then chances are that your site has hasn't been indexed yet.

The other database is used as a back up in case your search doesn't yield anything on the first. I haven't seen any updates on this index for quite sometime. There are indications from the technical staff that they will be merging the databases "sometime soon." I doubt this, as the Open Directory is quite comprehensive and is maintained by a separate entity.

Another doorway into Lycos is through their MP3 search engine. If you have songs in this format, then you can submit them to their MP3 section. Visit *Lycos Music* at **http://music.lycos.com** to find out more.

Webcrawler – http://www.webcrawler.com: previously the main search engine for AOL. Excite now has that honor. Still, Webcrawler is a useful search engine. To see your site's progress, enter in the URL(s) you submitted.

Human Driven:

Open Directory – http://www.dmoz.org: is a new breed of search engine. Each category is maintained by a "reviewer" that decides if your site is worthy of his/her category. The database maintained by this organization is also used by other search engines, like Lycos. There is no guarantee of how long it will take your site to be accepted. In addition, a reviewer is not obligated to notify you of entry. To see if your site was added, enter in the URL you submitted. You can expect the same result with About.com. However, their reviewers are a bit more fickle.

Yahoo! – http://www.yahoo.com: Is number one and has the reputation of being the most difficult to get a listing in. It was the first popular search engine and has become so impacted, that users are only allowed to "suggest" a site - not add one. Their staff actively checks the quality and content of a site before adding it to their index. Having a useful and professional looking web site can increase your chances in achieving the highly coveted Yahoo! listing. Yahoo! is selective because they are trying to provide quality content to surfers. Unless your site has a significant amount of content or plays a pivotal roll in the online world, your site has slim or little chance in getting listed in Yahoo!. However, if you choose to pursue a listing, make sure that you read their submission instructions carefully and follow them to the letter. The Yahoo! directory editors will contact you when your site is accepted. The next chapter, *To Yahoo! or Not to Yahoo!* steps you through their detailed submission process.

Frequently Asked Submission Questions

How often should I resubmit?
Resubmit only when your ranking lowers dramatically or disappears. A significant drop in traffic for more than a few days is a strong sign that your rankings have dropped.

How can I tell whether my pages have been listed yet?
You can do it the hard way by using the "Check Status" feature on some search engines, for example Infoseek, or you can use position analysis software. The simplest way is to search on different combinations of your keywords with your domain name in various search engines.

META keywords tag - should I use UPPERCASE or lowercase? commas or spaces?
Always use lowercase, separated by commas. Spaces in phrases are okay. Here is an example:

"vocalist,singer,songwriter,keyboardist,free mp3s"

Will I get penalized for having the same word repeated in phrases within my keyword list?
For example:

```
<META NAME="keywords" CONTENT="lead singer,lead vocalist,lead guitarist,leader of the pack">
```

The word *lead* - even in *leader* - counts as four repetitions. You will get penalized.

How about using forwarding pages with the REFRESH tag?
For example:

```
<META HTTP-EQUIV=REFRESH CONTENT="0; URL=http://www.domain.com/trick.html">
```

Spiders and robots from deep search engines spotted this trick ages ago. Don't do it. If you want diversity in a search engine, submit all of your sub-pages and design the keywords of each to reflect the content.

What about frames?
Avoid them if you can. Some deep engines have difficulty with them. If you're HTML savvy, use the <NO FRAMES> tag.

What is the most number of pages I can submit at one time?
It depends on the search engine. Limit the number of submissions to no more than 10 pages over a twenty-four hour period. However, do not submit the same page more than once, within this period.

TIME TO CHECK IN:

• Double Check Every Page

❏ Make Your Keywords "Fit" Each Page
"Tune" each page for the intended audience - fans, press, A&R reps - by reordering or adding keywords.

❏ <META> Description Says "WHY"
Word your description to say why surfers should drop by - free music, contest, etc.

❏ <TITLE>s Read Like a Headline
A Title is displayed in most search engines first like a newspaper headline. Write your titles in the same manner.

• Submit To The Top Six Deep Search Engines

❏ AltaVista
www.altavista.com/av/content/addurl.htm

❏ Lycos
www.lycos.com/addasite.html

❏ Infoseek
www.infoseek.com/AddUrl?pg=DCaddurl.html

❏ Excite
www.excite.com/info/add_url

❏ Hot Bot
www.hotbot.com/addurl.asp

❏ Web Crawler
www.webcrawler.com/Help/GetListed/AddURLS.html

- **Prepare Descriptions For Other Engines**

  ❏ Subject Specific Directories
  > You will have to manually enter the Title and Descriptions in your META tags with these search engines. Save yourself some work by keeping your titles, descriptions, and keyword lists in a text file. This will enable you to cut and paste them in Directories and Human Driven Engines.

  ❏ Yahoo! (Covered In Next Chapter) and the Open Directory
  > Same deal here. I know it sucks….but the mice are separated from the men this way.

  ❏ Save In Plain Text File For Later Use
  > Add what you submitted to your plain text file.

- **Submit To Subject Specific Directories**

  ❏ Music Yellow Pages
  > www.musicyellowpages.com

  ❏ MuseNet
  > www.musenet.com

  ❏ Search for More Music Related Sites
  > There are more in the *Internet Resources* section. Once you have exhausted the list, go to your favorite search engine and do a search.

GET READY TO Yahoo!

NOTES:

NOTES:

NOTES:

NOTES:

CHAPTER 10

To Yahoo! or Not to Yahoo!

Yahoo! is a special case and has the reputation of being the single most difficult directory to get an entry in. While there is not a perfect method to becoming a member of this exclusive directory, you can take measures to increase your chances. Unlike deep search engines with spider technology, *Yahoo! is human driven. This is how they have managed to stay ahead of the other competing search engines.*

Yahoo! is overwhelmed by add requests. Without human intervention, the quality of information on their site would rapidly deteriorate. To combat this, Yahoo! employs a staff of web surfers whose only job is to review web sites. These professional surfers review hundreds of sites each day and look for a winning combination. They reject 70% of the add requests received. If Yahoo! is so difficult to get into then "why bother" you say? Consider this, Yahoo! is responsible for more than half of the traffic in web commerce. To put it plainly, if you are going to sell music online, Yahoo! is the most lucrative listing you can achieve.

There is still hope. Alta Vista and Yahoo! joined forces in 1996 when they saw each other rising in popularity. Instead of competing with each other, they decided to become partners. As a result, Yahoo! then assimilated deep search engine characteristics. When a listing is not found on Yahoo! it transparently searches on Alta Vista. Until you can get a categorized listing on Yahoo!, a submission to Alta Vista will at least add you to the bottom of the ranks.

Basic Requirements for Yahoo! to Consider Your Site

A Finished Site

Do not submit your site if any part of it is under construction. An unfinished site is of no use to anyone and reviewers will ignore it for consideration into their category.

Content

Yahoo! wants useful sites for their users. Your site must have value. By offering free music or having contests, you make your site unique *and* valuable to Yahoo!'s visitors. If your band is associated with a local or seasonal event, your chances of getting into the Yahoo! directory are greater.

Design

If a page looks unorganized, loads slowly, or just appears amateurish it will most likely be ignored.

Size Does Matter

A single-page site has less of a chance getting listed than a multi-page site. Also, your press kit will show that you are media savvy.

Stay Within the Lines

Choose only a category and keywords that are appropriate to your Web site. Cleverness won't get you anywhere. Yahoo! site reviewers have seen it all.

If you don't follow these simple guidelines and if by the off chance your site is accepted, you will get a bad Yahoo! listing. Once you are in Yahoo! it is difficult to change any part of your listing. Even though there is a "Change URL" form, it is infamous for being ignored! Be absolutely sure that you are ready to submit!

Submitting to Yahoo!

Step One - Categories

Yahoo! allows submission to two categories; one primary and one secondary. Search in Yahoo! for the keyword at the top of your list and select the category that best fits. Once inside the category start your submission by clicking the "Add URL" graphic.

Step Two - Title

Enter the text in the <TITLE> tag of the page being submitted. Yahoo! does not automatically use this tag like deep search engines. You will have to type it in the submission form manually. If you have crafted your <TITLE> as recommended in *Search Engine Secrets* then all you have to do is copy it into Yahoo!'s "AddUrl" form.

Step Three - Description

The Yahoo! description and <META> description in your page are unrelated. The official maximum length of a Yahoo! description is around 25 words. Other search engines are more generous. You may have to shorten your <META> description and enter it into the submission form. Practically it should be even shorter because Yahoo! is notorious for chopping descriptions short.

You can find out how much you can get away with by taking a look at the listings in your chosen primary category. Ideally a description should be a single natural sentence avoiding the use of commas. Try to include your top <META> keywords. Anything longer may be chopped off.

Step Four - URL

Yahoo! is the only search engine where URL has relevancy to ranking! Although this factor is the least important, one can append keywords to a site's URL to help Yahoo! reviewers place your site in an appropriate category:

*http://www.tacotruffles.com/**music**/**web**/**design**/index.html.*

Step Five - Comments

Help Yahoo! reviewers by describing the benefits of your site to their audience. If you are giving away free music, sponsored by an organization, etc., let them know in a professional rhetoric. This shows that you are all business and your web site contributes to the "natural good" of cyberspace. Yahoo! wants quality content. Because your site is most likely an *official artist site*, it is important that you show reviewers you are not just another small-stage hack.

A Few Final Thoughts

Even the best sites have never received a primary category in Yahoo! but don't be discouraged. You may have better luck in Yahoo!'s regional listings for your geographical area. Yahoo!'s staff may award you with a regional listing, especially if your site looks active and represents your region well.

Don't let Yahoo! stop you from promoting yourself aggressively. I have seen it take as long as four attempts over a five month period and as little as one try in two weeks, to get listed in Yahoo! Keep trying. Yahoo! reviewers are telling you that your site is not offering anything useful to their readers by denying you entrance. There are still many more ways to get the word out. So let's *go for it!*

HEADS UP: Yahoo! does not have a link to add a new URL on their home page. Instead, one has to search on a keyword to find an applicable category for his/her site. Once inside a category, the AddURL link is available. Yahoo! embeds the AddURL link deep within to separate the pros from the amateurs.

TIME TO CHECK IN:

• Create A Page Designed To Yahoo!

❑ **Find the Appropriate Category**

Search on your keywords to find a category that suits you *and* your site. Click on the category and look at listings to get the "vibe." Click on AddURL graphic to begin submission process

❑ **Find An Alternate Category**

Search on your other keywords to find more categories.

❑ **Use Keywords in URL**

Based on your primary category, create directories on your site and place your Yahoo! enhanced HTML document there. For example, your category is composer: *www.myband.com/music/composer/yahoo.html*. This will help the Yahoo! staff place your site correctly.

❑ **Draft A One Line Description**

Your <META> description is not used by Yahoo! So you will have to draft a short 25 (or less) word statement that tells surfers why they should visit your site.

• Submit Your Special Page to Yahoo!

❑ **Try the Main Directory**

Sit back and wait for a few weeks. You may not get added. Remember, 70% of all submissions are denied.

❑ **Try the Local Directory**

If a few weeks go by and your submission is not in Yahoo!, try the "local" Yahoo! listings. They have one for most metropolitan areas.

❑ **Try Events**

If you're still not getting in, you can squeeze in the back door, especially if you are a part of a onetime or seasonal event.

❑ **Try Try Again**

Still didn't make it? Hone your site and make it better! Try all over again!

NOTES:

NOTES:

CHAPTER 11

Where Does The Money Come From?

Digital music distribution on the Internet has enabled independent artists to increase their visibility while keeping a larger share of the profits. It has also made it possible for independent labels to use new business models. In this chapter, we are going to explore one of the most common business models – the artist as the independent songwriter - and where the money comes from.

As with any business, it is important to know where the money comes from and where it is going. The traditional methods of collecting royalties by Performance Right Organizations and various other transactions are in their "online" infancy. However, some alliances have been forged that are paving the way for tracking sales, performances, and distribution. In order to understand how things have to change to make a similar mechanism work online, let's take a look at how the existing flow of money works offline.

Traditional Model - Simplified

In the traditional offline model, money mainly flows from royalties collected by various agencies to publishers and then on down to the copyright holder of a song. These royalties include Mechanical, Performance, Sync, and Print. All other monies tend to flow through a record label and then on down to the artist/songwriter. All the while, each entity takes a percentage. To make following the money trail easier, let's assume that the artist is also the songwriter. Let's also say that the artist is signed with a small label that handles distribution, touring, and owns half of the publishing. The "offline model" on the next page shows the flow of money based on retail sales of an artist's CDs, airplay, and live performances.

Performance Royalties are collected by Performance Right Organizations (PRO), like ASCAP, BMI, and SESAC for songs played on radio, television, film, and live performances. Once you sign with a publisher or label, ownership of your songs becomes open to negotiation. The chart on the following page assumes a "co-publishing" deal of 50/50. Any monies collected are paid to the publisher and songwriter separately. Any public use of your song is considered a "performance", i.e. television, radio, film, elevators, business, and other public spaces. These all generate performance royalties on your behalf. This is why it is extremely important to file your copyright and then register your work with a PRO.

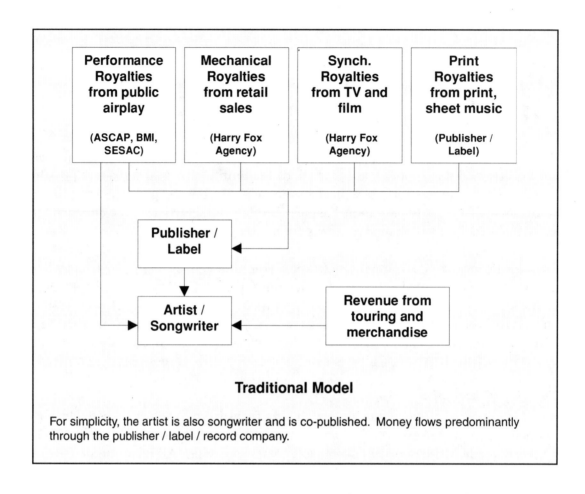

Traditional Model

For simplicity, the artist is also songwriter and is co-published. Money flows predominantly through the publisher / label / record company.

Mechanical royalties are collected by the Harry Fox Agency for the reproduction of a recorded song onto different media. This only includes CDs, tapes, and records – not audio files. Each instance or copy of a song generates 7.5 cents. Initially there was confusion over whether a downloaded file should be considered a copy of an original work or a performed work – i.e. streaming and webcasting. Although this was never formally settled, ASCAP made the leap first by seeking out online venues and granting them blanket licenses. So far, both downloaded and streamed audio files are considered as a public performance.

The money gathered for Mechanicals comes by tracking UPC codes through retail sales of recordings (SoundScan). This is why it is important to have a "proper and registered" UPC code on your product, to ensure that mechanical royalties are being collected and disseminated. Mechanical royalties are to be paid to the registered owner of the UPC code on the CD. That means that the UPC code represents the "registered" owner of the physical product. If you use someone else's or another company's UPC code, then you may be relinquishing the ownership of your CDs and forfeiting your Mechanical royalties.

Synchronization Royalties come from the licensing of a song for use in television or film. Your publisher negotiates the fee and regulates what is considered fair use of your work, while the Harry Fox Agency collects royalties. How this money is split depends on your contract. If you are not published, all of the money goes into your pocket and it is up to you to negotiate the use of your work. Last but not least, Print Royalties come from the reproduction of you songs on sheet music. Unless you are published, your work is not very likely to be distributed as sheet music.

As you can see from the previous chart, a majority of the royalties are paid to the publisher, who then splits the rest with the writer. The only exception is that PROs actually pay the songwriter their share directly. As long as the artist/songwriter remains independent, all royalties belong to him or her. However, this may not be in the best interest of your career. Each cut on your royalties goes to paying someone for furthering your music career. Well…ideally.

How Does It Work Online?

Royalties are still collected by PROs. After their cut is taken out, the leftovers are split between the publisher and the copyright owner. Performance royalties can now come from Internet Radio casts, Web Casts, downloaded songs, and offline radio stations that stream their signals online as well. Artists can also sell, CDs, merchandise, and digital audio files directly to fans from their own web site, effectively acting as a distributor and bypassing their label or publisher.

With the Internet, the artist/songwriter is at the center of everything. Although a major label still offers many valuable business related services and has many strong advantages, an artist can still get online and "bypass" traditional business partners to sell their own songs, cuts, mixes, merchandise, and even make use of a different online distributor. However, because major artists typically sign away all of their rights, major labels can prevent and even discourage major artists from getting online to gain exposure. As an independent artist, nothing can hold you back but yourself. *Cyberlaw* discusses this in greater detail.

Money, It's a Hit.

Major labels are still concerned about piracy and ensuring that "digital distributors" and webcasters are registered and monitored in a effective manner that will ensure all royalties are collected. While a major artist can be prevented from using the Internet, an independent artist can develop their own promotion campaign and music persona on-the-fly. Take a look at the following chart. Notice that the artist is at the center of everything. This is because an artist can essentially pick any service that works best for them.

Most labels have not yet effectively inserted themselves into the online scene to provide the services needed to assist their artists with online exposure. This has led to their general discouragement of major artists, in essence to prevent them, from bypassing labels until the industry can come up with a secure method of using the Internet while using it as a new medium of exposure.

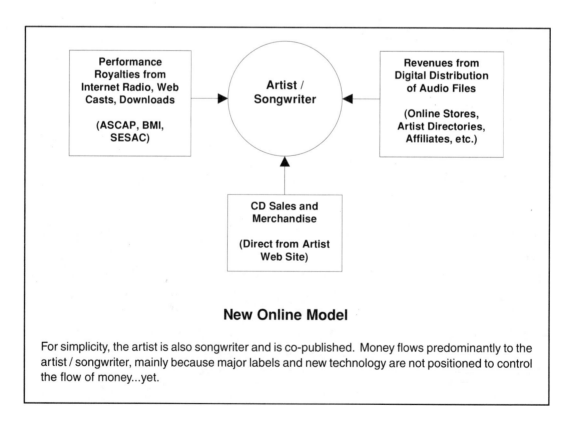

New Online Model

For simplicity, the artist is also songwriter and is co-published. Money flows predominantly to the artist / songwriter, mainly because major labels and new technology are not positioned to control the flow of money...yet.

Hear Today, Royalties Tomorrow?

The Internet is still a widely unregulated entity. Not only have PROs been grappling with it, so has the music industry – the Big Five: BMG, EMI, Sony, AOL Time-Warner, and the Universal Music Group. So far there has been an uneasy alliance between online stores, artists directories, Internet radio and webcasters, the various performance right organizations, and the record industry. They acknowledge each other but are not working well together online. This is mainly because the "new media" of the Internet is still considered separate from the "old media" of television, radio, and print. The Internet for a long while was actually considered a "fad" by many of the top people in the industry. With the merging of AOL and Time-Warner, this mentality is sure to change in the near future.

For example, ASCAP and MP3.com agreed on a license fee that is paid on a regular basis and then disseminated to artists based on sales and downloads of songs. This does not benefit BMI and SESAC artists. The RIAA successfully lobbied to provide licensing of Internet Radio stations that is backed by laws different than those that govern traditional broadcast radio. *CyberLaw* will cover this detail.

On the other hand, Emusic is a prime example of the future of cooperation between every facet of the offline model translated online. It is affiliated with all of the PROs and is considered part of the record industry. Liquid Audio has also positioned itself as an online distributor through their Liquid Platinum program.

Quick Royalty Review

Performance Royalties - accrue from radio or public airplay in jukeboxes, stores, etc. (Performance Right Organizations like ASCAP, BMI, SESAC)

Mechanical Royalties - are collected from Retail Sales (Harry Fox Agency).

Synchronization Royalties - come from the use of your songs in television or movies (Harry Fox Agency)

Sampling Royalties - come from using snippets of your work in other artist's songs. (Your Publisher or Label)

Print Royalties - comes from when your song is printed in books, magazines, or sheet music. (Your Publisher or Label)

Digital Distribution – i.e. No Labels

Another great fear of the record industry has been that their artists will be able to sell music without a label. Primarily because they no longer have control over the distribution of them. This is largely unfounded. Major labels still provide a great many other services and financial benefits that an online store or artist site can not do without, i.e. touring, press, promotion.

This is why the Recording Industry Association of America (RIAA) formed the Secure Digital Music Initiative (SDMI). SDMI's function is to moderate third party companies that manufacture products aiding in the securing of music distribution online.

By controlling how companies develop hardware and software to distribute music, the record industry can be assured that a majority of the money will flow back to them. However, there is an advantage to this. Because third party companies are developing technology to aid in the secure distribution of music, they are making their services available to independent artists. Until the majors can organize the "troops" online, it will continue to be difficult to track the flow of revenue online for both independent and major artists. This will allow you to turn the record industry's weaknesses into your strengths.

TIME TO CHECK IN:

You Get a Break This Chapter

Take this time to review your overall strategy.

You have made one, right?!

NOTES:

CHAPTER 12

CyberPrise: Thinking E-Commerce

In this chapter, we are going to explore the different ways to get your music into new channels of distribution and how to "move" product online. We will also examine other gimmicks to sell more CDs from your web site.

So far, we have explored getting online, promoting your web site and generating publicity for it. There is a good reason for this. What we have been doing up to this point is creating a hub from which you can effectively promote your music and support other sites that carry your "product." Now is the time to venture out into cyberspace to find places to put your songs.

Venturing Into Cyberspace

There are millions of people online primarily interested in music alone. However, they are most likely not looking for your web site. Instead, they are looking for web sites with the latest, greatest music. This means that you have to get your music into these venues and cross promote your site with them.

With so many different types of venues on the Internet, it can be hard to tell what you are getting yourself into. Some only deal in sound files, others drop ship your CD, and there are even full blown record labels that will handle your promotion and distribution online. Many of these venues you to sign a contract to authorize distribution of your work - all of them should.

Life Beyond Search Engines and MP3.com

To help you put things into perspective, let's categorize the online venues that can carry your music in a variety of forms – CD, digital audio, custom mixes, etc. Let's start with more traditional forms of business related to the Internet; drop shippers:

Drop Shippers: come in a variety of sizes. They store a few of your CDs in their warehouse and process orders for you, enabling you to accept credit cards. There are small ones that cater only to independent artists and then there are the incredibly large companies, like Amazon.com, that will carry almost anything and everything. Many of the large Drop Shippers require that your CD have a registered UPC code. Others offer a UPC code as "bonus" for using their service.

Be careful of this. While this is a nice thing that they do for you, keep in mind that the UPC code is under their name, technically making your CD their property. Any monies collected from mechanical royalties, sales, etc. goes to the owner of the UPC code. This means that they are responsible for reimbursing you the money that is collected by offline stores, like Borders, Tower, etc. Already, one known Internet distributor and their business partner have gotten into hot water over the UPCs they have provided for "free."

- **CD Baby – http://www.cdbaby.com:** The most reputable drop shipper catering to independent artists. I recommend you start here if you don't have a UPC code. They have good turnaround time and are popular overseas. You get a personalized page and the benefit of their customer service dealing with customers directly.

- **Amazon.com – http://www.amazon.com:** will carry your CD as long as it has a UPC code. They take a bigger piece of your sales than CD Baby. However, it would be a good idea to place your product on one of the most trusted online music and book retailers. Their program is called the *Amazon Advantage* and they pay you directly *every month*.

- **CDNow – http://www.cdnow.com:** is the first online record store to be hugely successful. They too require a UPC code. However, they are not as well known as Amazon.com. Most customers that visit CDNow are not looking for independent music. Their main focus is on major artists and older product. CDNow can be last on your list of places to have your CD drop shipped.

- **The Orchard – http://www.theorchard.com:** claims to get your CD into Amazon.com, CDNow, Music Boulevard, and the Valley Music catalog (VMC), which is used by many of the online stores as a product list. Even though the Orchard, in essence, gets you "in" these sites, it is not what you think. *Special Note:* when you get a listing in Amazon.com or CDNow, using the Orchard, your CD does not have a description of it, sound samples and is shown as "on back order," which discourages most customers from ordering. There is also more UPC hilarity with this "service." *Another Special Note*: Valley Music is one of the largest distributors to traditional "brick and mortar" record stores. Having a listing in their catalog does not mean stores will carry your CD or that they will ever order it.

Meta Sites: are web sites that act as "music portals" or huge online song catalogs that allow consumers to buy music on a song-by-song basis, entire CD, or both. Meta Sites are typically categorized by genre and sometimes by geographic area. It can be very difficult to be found in these sites among the tens of thousands of other artists. MP3.com is the most well known of this kind of venue. There are new Meta Sites popping up everyday and it would be impossible to put them all in this book. Visit our site to find a list of more venues in this vein – **http://IndiePromo.com/venues**. For now, here are the more reputable web sites that offer a lot of ears for your music to be heard.

- **MP3.com – http://www.mp3.com:** splits all sales with you 50/50 and lets you set the price of your songs. They offer the benefit of burning your CDs for you (D.A.M. or Digital Audio Music CD) and mailing them off to purchasers. Your contract with them can be canceled anytime by either you or them. All you have to do is provide the MP3 files, a bio, cover art, and a picture for your listing. You can upload all of your songs or entire albums and group them in any way like. It is entirely flexible. You have complete control over which songs you want to have available for free and which ones are only available on the custom CD. *Special Note:* MP3.com carries songs from thousands of artists. Don't be fooled into thinking that potential fans go there to find "new music." Much of the traffic are the Artists directing their fans to their MP3.com "site." Also, don't be fooled that if you are on their "top downloads" chart that it will result in thousands of CD sales. Many artists on MP3.com confess they have regularly downloaded their song to increase their chart position. I have never met an artist that has made more than a very small fistful of dollars (if that) from their MP3.com listing.

- **Rolling Stone Magazine – http://www.rollingstone.com:** wants independent artists to upload their music in MP3 format. There you can get your music heard by the industry and even reviewed by their staff. They rate the top 10 most promising songs every month. You can also get a personalized page there with your lyrics, tour schedule, bio and photos, and even track the number of downloads of your work.

- **StompinGround.com – http://www.stompinground.com:** is a smaller version of MP3.com. This makes it much easier to be found and allows them to offer more personalized service. They connect fans to artists by giving reviews of newly submitted music and are devout independent music fans. Stompinground.com also focuses their efforts on attracting A&R reps and industry professionals to their site.

Artist Directories: are similar in nature to Meta Sites but typically lean more towards providing services for the artist, i.e. free web sites, email, and audio file storage.

- **Internet Underground Music Archive (IUMA) - http://www.iuma.com:** is a web directory that has over 20,000 music fans every day looking for independent acts. It used to cost a lot of money ($240 US) to get a single page with a photo, bio, and one song. Emusic bought them out, and as a result, IUMA is now a free service. *Special Note*: Keep the thoughts of MP3.com artists in mind. You have to tell people you are there. Very, very few people are surfing through hundreds of "look alike" pages to "find" something new.

- **Ultimate Band List (UBL) - http://www.ubl.com:** is a smaller version of IUMA and is growing fast. It is free and gets a lot of traffic. Your listing allows a bio, your existing email address, and a link to your "official" web page. UBL doesn't provide a means for fans to hear your music. So you still need a Web page of your own to take advantage of this free service.

- **IndieGroup – http://www.indiegroup.com:** is also known as the Circle of Independence. It is an affiliation between some heavy independent hitters, like TAXI, The Orchard, Band Utopia, MusicPromotion.net, GetSigned.com, and MusicDish, to name a few. They all offer services that empower artists everywhere. There you can get free email and web pages to get your band up on the Internet ASAP. Between all of them, you can find ezines and publications to get your music reviewed, clubs and venues to perform in, indie industry news, software, classifieds, and a whole lot more.

How Meta Sites & Artist Directories Can Hinder Your Career

Keep in mind that with Meta Sites, you have no control over the design and layout of your "page." Your free page is nothing more than a generic template. This will make it difficult to stand out among the masses and to create the appropriate mood to match your music. However, the potential to generate traffic to your "official" site is tantalizing. Meta Sites and Artist Directories, along side a full blown Web page, will increase your presence on the web and allow you to update your information effortlessly.

The New Frontier: Digital Distribution and CyberLabels

Digital Distribution and Affiliates: This is where the big guys are breaking ground for both the big and small artist. You can bet the merger between AOL and Time-Warner will open up new avenues in this segment of e-commerce. For now, there is only one affiliate program of great note:

- **Liquid Platinum - http://www.liquidmusicnetwork.com:** This is a relatively new service that is driven by Liquid Audio's technology. For $99US per year, you can get your music into some 350 (and growing) affiliates. The best part is that you don't have to do anything but make music, get your CD into this system, and provide some basic information about you. This is going to be the wave of the future because the affiliates spend a lot of money attracting consumers to their sites. The best part is that your songs will have built in security measures to prevent piracy. This is also the same technology that the record industry supports. Contact Liquid Audio right away to find out who the affiliates are. *Special Note:* This program also offers "verifiable" accounting that you can show to other companies, such as record labels and publishers, how your success is growing.

Record Labels: Internet record labels are popping up everywhere. They typically split revenue from sales with the artist 50/50. This is similar to the *Amazon Advantage* program that Amazon.com provides. Some labels also share in the revenue generated by advertising, in lieu of record sales. However, just like a traditional label, an Internet record label should be putting additional effort behind your record – i.e. promotion, distribution, etc.

The line between Meta Sites and Internet record labels is often blurred. Many labels also double as online music stores where their featured artists' music can be downloaded in MP3 and/or purchased in the more traditional physical formats like CDs and cassettes. Here are some of the more widely known Internet record labels.

- **AMP3.com:** sells downloadable music and pays artists up to 50 cents every time one of their songs is downloaded. Sponsors pay anywhere from 10 to 20 cents per download to place ads at the beginning of songs. Consumers have the option of downloading songs for free or purchasing the songs with the ads removed. This is an example of where the revenue generated from advertising is split with the artist.

- **Emusic.com:** was formerly known as GoodNoise.com and is one of the more well known online record labels/music distributors. Through relationships with artists and license agreements with leading independent record labels, Emusic.com offers a wide variety of downloadable music in the MP3 format. This online resource is also licensed with the major PROs. More royalties for the artist!

- **MP3.com:** is not a record label! MP3.com may distribute your music, but does not offer any promotion of your music other than to get visitors to their site. Remember, there are already over 40,000 artists there. You can not possibly stand out among them.

What to Look Out for Before You Sign With Any Label

The same holds true for your online presence as it does offline; distribution does little or no good without promotion. Be sure to ask any self-proclaimed "record label" if they provide promotion of their artists and what kind. Many only provide promotion for the label's own web page and interests. Labels like these foolishly believe that if they get enough visitors to their site, all of their artists will benefit from exposure. So be sure to stay on top of their online and offline promotion efforts. Insist that they allow you to erect your own web site and cross-promote it with theirs - i.e. promotion dollars for both sites.

Since Internet labels have not proven themselves offline, as well as online, control your music by only letting them "sell it" on their site for a percent of sales. Do not give them full control of your music! In fact, if you have more than one CD, you can shield the rest of your work, by only authorizing a label to "sell" one of your CDs or downloadable audio files, until they prove what they can do. Talk with other artists, regarding their experience with these sites. Remember, *your perception of something good is not always reality of the way it really is.* (*CyberLaw* discusses more of the potential legal and professional problems that can arise when dealing with online entities like labels and Internet radio.)

A Few Ideas to Convert Traffic Into $$$'s At Your Own Site

Now that we have covered many ways to get your songs placed in different venues, we still need to discuss different ways to handle the traffic driven to your site from other affiliates and how to increase impulse buys. If you are accepting credit cards and willing to process orders, you could increase your sales with the following methods from your site:

- **Free Song + Upgrade:** Offer a special mix of one of your singles in MP3 format for free, then offer or "up sell" your CD with the "full" or "radio" version.

- **Trial CD:** Offer your CD on a two-week trial basis and collect the money later. This may result in some fans not owning up to the bill, but you will certainly move a lot more CDs this way, where the majority who receive your product will pay up. You can also use Liquid Audio's "dissolve" feature on your hit song to "entice" fans to download your music and then, when the files "expire," a pop-up banner will inform the fans to buy your full CD or to purchase songs, individually. Otherwise, your music will be erased by the Liquid Audio file player. *Protecting Music Online* covers more methods to control distribution of your music.

- **Subscription:** Charge a monthly fee to access special photos, songs, and late breaking news. Only famous folks have had moderate success with this model, like David Bowie and Todd Rundgren. You could conceivably do this for a special event – i.e. a video web cast, live casts, etc. for fans abroad.

It is still possible to accept checks and money orders with these methods, but the time and effort it would take to process orders and collect monies would not make it worth your while. Internet billing services, such as CCNow and IBill, would be the best solution for this situation; otherwise ask if your record label will process credit cards and fulfill orders for you.

The Future of Music Distribution

Right now the record industry is scrambling to get secure distribution in place. They will eventually succeed. Secure music distribution will evolve to be as much a part of the online landscape as shipping and credit card processing services, and, as a result, will offer consumers more flexibility in purchasing their favorite music.

Systems currently under development will include music subscription services where you pay a flat monthly fee to listen to an unlimited amount of music, or micro-payments, where your account is charged a small amount each time you listen to a song. I just hope that a 21st century equivalent to a record club doesn't start sending me music I know I didn't order!

Other systems under development will emphasize a "rent-to-own" business model, where consumers can listen to a song a fixed number of times for a small fee and purchase more "listens" when the limit is reached. After a specified number of "listens" are purchased, the song is "owned" by the consumer. Of course, there will always be the option to buy a song or the entire album right off. Whether or not this system will be well received is another matter.

Other potential systems will let you download a song and listen to it for free for a limited number of times or period (week, month, etc.), after which you must purchase a key-code to enable the song for permanent use. With such a system, songs can be e-mailed by fans to their friends for a "demo" period, until they too purchase a unique code-key. Liquid Audio offers this capability - **http://www.liquidmusicnetwork.com**.

No doubt, the record industry has finally come to terms with the power of the Internet and is undergoing a major change. A day will come when, instead of going to a record store, you will go to a kiosk or "music station," much like a soda vending machine, to download music into a handheld device or receptacle. How any of these new distribution systems will take hold is a question of whether or not consumers will "buy it." As music consumers ourselves, we will be able to shape the way the industry does business by voting with our wallets and encouraging our fans to do so, too.

TIME TO CHECK IN:

• **Place Your CDs Into Key CyberSpace Depots**

❑ CD Baby
www.cdbaby.com

❑ The Orchard
www.theorchard.com
Decide whether you want them to distribute to Amazon.com, CDNow, and Music Boulevard for you, or go to them individually to provide your music with the expanded look and feel that you want

• **Place Your Hit Songs Into Online Stores & Meta Sites**

❑ MP3.com
www.mp3.com

❑ Rolling Stone Magazine
www.rollingstone.com

❑ Stompinground.com
www.stompinground.com

❑ Liquid Platinum (350+ Online Stores for $99/yr!)
www.liquidmusicnetwork.com

❑ Find More Online Stores & Meta Sites in Search Engines

• **Place Your Hit Songs and Information Into Artist Directories**

❑ The Ultimate Band List (UBL)
www.ubl.com

❑ Internet Underground Music Archive (IUMA)
www.iuma.com

❑ IndieGroup
   www.indiegroup.com

• Find an Internet Record Label That Fits Your Promotion Campaign

❑ AMP3.com
   www.amp3.com

❑ Emusic.com
   www.emusic.com

❑ Find More Labels in Search Engines and at IndiePromo.com
   Remember, you can "sign" with as many record labels as you like, as long as you
   don't give away all of your distribution rights. Make sure you know what you are
   getting into before you sign anything.

• Adopt A Business Model For Selling CDs & Merchandise Direct From Your Site

❑ Pick One
   Free Song + Upgrade
   Trial CD Offer
   Subscription – offer this only if you have a large and extremely loyal fan base

NOTES:

NOTES:

NOTES:

NOTES:

Reality Check: Thinking "E-Commercial"

The Internet is redefining how traditional business is done. By getting a firm hold online now, position yourself in a way that enables you to implement new technology, monitor online trends and redefine marketing strategies. While major labels are downsizing, fighting piracy and trying to gain a foothold online, you can completely revamp your promotion campaign. However, time is still short, as the music industry is working hard to catch up.

Even though you have a site on the Web, mastered search engines, sent out press releases and gig regularly, you will only reach a small percentage of the online population. However, new resources pop-up everyday, while old ones fade away. That is why it is important to spend a little time every week to educate yourself on trends, by using search engines to find new resources and to "network" online. This is a key point where many artists fall short. The next section, *Creating Online & Offline Publicity for Your Music*, will show you how to ensure your online and offline longevity.

Creating Online & Offline Publicity for Your Music

CHAPTER 13

Internet Radio and Online Publicity

When starting out, it is essential to create traffic to your web site through multiple publicity channels. Many artists fail to realize that it is not enough to erect a web site and submit to search engines. That is only a tiny part of a successful online campaign. In order to create a buzz, potential fans and visitors have to be "herded" to your site. In this chapter, we are going to explore the many ways you can generate publicity online through Internet Radio, Ezines, email, and other electronic media.

How Online Publicity Differs from Offline Publicity

Essentially, the motives of online publicity are the same as offline publicity. The major difference is that it can cost almost nothing. With offline publicity, there are constant expenses in telephone calls, faxes, shipping and handling, and cranking out demos. You can curb most of this by finding labels and publications that accept online submissions – usually the small guys. One advantage with an online press kit is that, A&R reps and the media can see what kind of buzz you are generating online easier than in person. They can read your guest book and see what fans are saying, view your press kit and listen to your work. Plus, you can introduce new material in a matter of moments and on a regular basis. No agent can provide that kind of service twenty-four hours a day, year-round, and especially worldwide. To start, let's take a look at all of the opportunities that Internet Radio has to offer.

Internet Radio

Internet Radio represents a new era where consumers can control the media instead of the other way around. This is because traditional radio is not an interactive medium. However, with Internet radio, listeners can give feedback and to some extent, control programming. This is only a natural evolution, as the Web is inherently interactive.

In addition, Internet radio grants access to a wider variety of programming than on traditional broadcast radio. Internet radio sites have anywhere between one to several hundreds of channels of programming containing different music, news, sports, talk radio…you name it. If it has sound, you can bet it has its own channel.

Most importantly, Internet radio is not bound by geography. It is international. When your music gets on any Internet Radio site, it's getting international exposure. Internet radio sites generate advertising revenue with not only on-air and banner ads, they can generate revenue from music related products sold through their sites, namely, your CD.

Unlike broadcast radio, Internet radio sites show the name of the artist, the title of the song, sometimes lyrics, and even your album graphic as your song is playing. Most importantly, they will either show where to buy your CD or sell it for you. The advantage to this is that if someone likes your song, they can buy it or the entire album while listening to your work, instead of having to track it down in online or offline stores. Traditional radio stations can't even come close to this kind of exposure. For the first time, an artist can receive revenue directly from radio exposure.

Where Can You Find the Perfect Internet Radio Exposure?

With a press kit and audio samples ready to roll online, you can increase your exposure by getting airplay and/or reviewed on Internet Radio shows. It is fast becoming the medium of choice and still has a lot of *indie* spirit. Most even accept unsolicited material and prefer indie artists. You can generate a lot of publicity and web traffic overnight with just a few spins. All it takes is a little homework to find the most appropriate site for your musical style.

MIT (Massachusetts Institute of Technology) maintains a web site that has a comprehensive list of regular and Internet Radio sites at **http://wmbr.mit.edu/stations**. There is also the Radio Directory, which is organized by geographical location. It's Internet Radio listings are growing and organized by continent, then by country and state – **http://www.radiodirectory.com/Stations**. IndiePromo.com has narrowed down its listings to Internet Radio sites looking for submissions. This is especially handy if you are trying to get your music on Internet radio ASAP or if you simply don't have the time to search for decent radio stations – **http://IndiePromo.com/ir**.

A Couple of Helping Hands

Internet radio sites are popping up all over the world, everyday, all with unique programming. The directories can not possibly keep up. Thankfully, there is a nifty program called MP3spy. With it you can search for Internet Radio sites that use a specific kind of MP3 streaming technology called SHOUTcast. All you have to do is set some criteria and let it do some trolling for you. With the least bit of effort, you can find sites that cater to specific genres and specialty programming.

You may find some specialty programming that is perfectly suited to songs that you thought could never be marketed. Visit **http://www.mp3spy.com** to get a copy of this stand-alone program. However, be aware that sites associated with SHOUTcast technology tend to be on the fringes of the law. If you are comfortable with getting airplay without any guarantee of royalties coming in from these stations, then this is the perfect watchdog for you. Keep in mind, for all of your effort, these more "questionable" stations may end up getting shutdown or go "out of business."

Another program based on the RealAudio technology is called vTunner. Even though this product is meant to be used by consumers, it too is another way to find thousands of radio stations and television programming from all over the world. vTunner comes in a free version that pummels you with advertisements. However, you can upgrade to the "plus" version that allows you to stop the ads ($29.99US) and add more functionality, such as scanning, playback scheduling, and station ratings based on programming quality and broadcast reliability. Visit: **http://www.vTunner.com** to download their interface program.

There are still countless nooks and crannies where MP3 files may be getting airplay. Scour.net is a great way to find some of the more obscure places to place your music. It is an MP3 search engine that can find MP3 files, videos, images, and all sorts of other types of audio and multimedia files. The Scour homepage has listings for other sites where you can download music and listen to Internet radio. All are potential places to get your music heard. Another useful thing about this site is that, you can search by Artist and/or songs name and specific file types, enabling you to see if any of your work is floating around on the Internet. Scour also has the latest news on the progress of digital music distribution. However, the only drawback is that you have to install a "media manager" on your computer in order to download files.

Internet Radio Sites of Note: The Big Guys and a Lot of Little Guys

Internet radio stations come in a variety of "models." Many are broadcast radio stations that are just beginning to offer their regular programming via the Internet. There are even live radio stations that broadcast via Internet only. Sites such as Broadcast.com act as "aggregators" or distributors of streaming media programming and Web content for both traditional radio stations and Internet only radio stations. Other Internet radio sites allow listeners to select their own programming from an extensive list of songs.

These are the most common models. However, to help you narrow down your search and to keep you on track, you need to focus on Internet radio stations that connect fans and indie artists together with interactive programming – i.e. live or automated DJ's. Here is why.

Major players like AOL and Rolling Stone Magazine see the value in online broadcasting and have tried to make their mark. AOL's Spinner.com offers over 100 different channels or "stations" and a selection of more than 150,000 songs. Rolling Stone Radio features stations that play music selected by rocks stars, such as David Bowie, and other celebrities. Many of these larger sites also offer music charts, industry news, and other types of music-related content. Unfortunately, Spinner.com doesn't allow you to set up your own radio station or accept submissions from *independent artists*. However, there are plenty of little guys out there that can help you get exposure.

Two sites of note are Green Witch and World Music Radio. Green Witch is a huge supporter of the independent arts. Unlike many other Internet radio sites, they are mostly free of commercial ads. They also offer a wide variety of programming including college radio, talk radio, comedy, and even animal noises. All artists are asked to sign an online agreement before their work can be broadcasted. Visit: **http:// www.greenwitch.com**.

World Music Radio is another station with great integrity. They broadcast half of the day with live DJs and then repeat the programming for the other. They interact a great deal with their listeners and support independent music wholeheartedly. They also allow artists to give interviews and play live on one of their shows. Although their namesake is "world music," they are open to most kinds of music and have some of the most eclectic programming I've ever heard. Like every legitimate Internet radio station, they are required to obtain permission for each song they play. Check out their programming at: **http://www.worldmusicradio.com**.

Unlike many of the larger Internet radio sites, such as Spinner.com and vTunner.com, you don't have to install any special "tuners" along with RealAudio and MP3 players. Green Witch streams in both RealAudio and MP3, which only require you to install RealPlayer or WinAmp, respectively, on your system. World Music Radio transmits in RealAudio and WindowsMedia. These are the quality of sites that you want to shoot for when submitting your material.

How to Get Internet Radio DJ's to Play Your Songs

Send an email to the web master describing your music and a link to your kit (no attachments!) and ask for their help in where you fit into their programming. With their input, you could get multiple placements. Even if your music doesn't fall into any specific categories or you're a crossover artist, Internet Radio is one of the cheapest ways to get "airplay" and diversify your exposure.

Integrating Internet Radio With Your Web Site

Now that you know a little about what Internet radio is and where to find some quality sites to submit your hit songs, let's a take a brief look at how your web site should integrate with any exposure gained.

- **List all radio stations, broadcast and Internet, that play your music.** Include who and how to contact each station for requests. With Internet radio, it is easy enough to put the station's email address for requests and even a phone number, with country codes on your web site and in email you send to fans. Remember, the web is international! Don't forget to include information that makes it easy for out of country fans to contact you and your stations! Also, be sure to remind fans that online radio stations, by law, can not broadcast songs any sooner that one hour after their request.

  Unfortunately, Internet radio sites can not announce when an artist's songs are to be played. However, they are required to display an artist's song information, during playback, and are allowed to make "general" announcements to help with promotion efforts. Whether or not you get an interview, link to any station that makes mention of you or plays your songs. *Music and the New CyberLaw* covers the laws that govern Internet radio in greater detail.

- **Send out regular email messages** to fans letting them know which radio stations you are getting airplay on, which songs are getting played, and what album they are on. If it is broadcast radio, note the geographic area the station covers and include a link to their web site if they webcast. For Internet only, include a link to the site and what type of stream they cast in – i.e. RealAudio, MP3, WindowsMedia, etc. Also include, for every station, how to make requests for your songs. If the DJ has an email, place a link to it in your email like so: *mailto:djname@radiostationname.com*.

- **If you are getting interviewed on a radio show, ask the DJ or station manager for an archive copy and permission to make it available on your site for download.** This will add a "bonus" to your site. You can treat the archive file on your site as an event that can be promoted offline. Also, tell your fans to call in if the station will be taking calls during the interview.

What if you could control all of these situations to leverage even more exposure? Would you create your own Internet Radio station if it was possible? Want to know how to create your very own radio station? It's easy...

Creating Your Own Internet Radio Station

Live365 is a unique service that allows you to create your own radio station for free. Not only that, your radio station will be ASCAP licensed! As long as you follow *their guidelines*, you can place your music on their systems and encourage fans to listen to you while at work or on the computer at home! Visit: **http://www.live365.com** to sign up for your very own Internet radio station.

The Digital Millennium Copyright Act, which is covered in greater detail in *CyberLaw*, requires your station programming can not be less than three hours in length, assuming your "show" will be looped. That's a lot of material you will have to fill!

You can put up recordings of your performances, interviews, etc. You can set up mach interviews and impromptu performances for later broadcast on your "station." With some effort, you could easily create enough content to keep your fans up to date on your progress. You can ban together with other artists to create an online scene for your community. If you are on a label, you should be able to get permission to place their other artists' material on the radio station, as well. However you can work it out, cross promote the radio station on all of the artists and label's sites.

Another way to generate interest in your station is to sell ads to the venues you are performing in. Now you can have little commercials on your station announcing specials and prizes for the venues you perform in. However, existing laws prevent commercial announcements on nonprofit stations that have a "call to action." This means that you can say, "we are performing at Go-Go's Doll House of Rock," but you can't say, "we are performing and come out now," "buy our album," etc.

As long as you have the permission of every copyright holder and follow the program criteria governed by law, you are well within your rights to webcast any material from your station. Here are the guidelines translated into *plain English* from the Digital Millennium Copyright ACT, 17 U.S.C : § 114:

1. Your program **must not** be part of an "interactive service." In plain terms, this means that, you cannot perform sound recordings **within one hour** of a request by a listener or at a time designated by the listener.

2. In any three-hour period, you **should not** intentionally program more than three songs (and not more than two songs in a row) from the same recording; you **should not** intentionally program more than four songs (and not more than three songs in a row) from the same recording artist or anthology/box set.

3. Continuous looped programs **may not** be less than three hours long.

4. Rebroadcasts of programs **may** be performed at scheduled times as follows:

   - Programs of less than one-hour: no more than three times in a two-week period;
   - Programs longer than one hour: no more than four times in any two-week period.

5. You **should not** publish advance program guides or use other means to pre-announce when particular sound recordings will be played.

6. You **should** only broadcast sound recordings that are authorized for performance in the United States.

7. You **should** pass through (and not disable or remove) identification or technological protection information included in the sound recording (if any).

Even if you own the copyright to every work transmitted, these guidelines always apply. They are there to prevent any unscrupulous use of the Internet that facilitates pirating copyrighted work, and discourages distributing copyrighted material without regard for artists' right to earn royalties. However, I doubt that you will report yourself to the authorities!

Also, did you notice that you can't announce your play list? That may seem to be a huge obstacle but there is nothing stopping you from announcing your next gig, specials on merchandise, trivia, etc.! Even with these strict criteria, you can still create an incredible online persona that A&R reps are hungry for.

Plus, Internet Radio doesn't suffer from reception problems. Fans can listen to your music wherever they have Internet access – i.e. at work, home, and in the near future hand-held computers and cellular phones. However, even with all of this opportunity, the technology that supports Internet radio does have its shortcomings.

Internet Radio Shortcomings: Nothing That Technology and Time Can't Fix

The main factor limiting Internet radio is bandwidth or how much fidelity a streamed signal can have. The minimum needed for a CD quality stereo signal is ISDN (up to 128kbps), but the majority of users have much slower connections. Signals that transmit in Voice quality are usually well suited at slower connection speeds, but music quality is barely acceptable with connections slower than 56kbps (current modem speeds).

However, emerging technology is enabling Internet connections in the home with more than enough bandwidth for high-quality audio - DSL, cable modems, and satellite links (all connecting at 128kbps and higher). However, even with unlimited bandwidth, network congestion can cause problems during peak usage periods. These problems will eventually be solved, but it could be years before the majority of Internet users have fast enough connections to receive high fidelity audio.

Another problem is in the technology that is used to transmit signals through the Internet itself. Most streaming audio and video on the Internet is transmitted in a *unicast* mode, which is extremely inefficient. With unicast, each listener or viewer receives a separate stream. A station that has 300 users will send 300 copies of the same stream. Even if every user had a fast Internet connection, the current unicast technology could only handle a few million simultaneous listeners. Eventually this will be addressed, as the "old" media continues to blend with the "new" and big media corporations put their money into this problem.

Ezines

Ezines or "Electronic Magazines" are specific interest publications that are usually maintained by an individual or small group. Some are email based, some are web only, and many are both. In this section, we are going to focus on ezines that are looking for indie music. There are countless ezines to suit every musical style and range from the fully corporate funded, to the "we publish when feel like it."

These days, every major offline publication has an online branch. These usually have the same content as the printed publication. Of course, your chances of getting reviewed on a local or small ezine are greater. Before you spend a great deal of time digging up decent publications, get started using the extensive list of ezines at the Ultimate Band List web site and in the table on the next page. If you are hungry for more publications, visit the companion site to this book at **http://IndiePromo.com/ezines** to search by genre.

Once you have found the appropriate ezines for your songs, send an email to the editor. Just like with Internet Radio, describe your music and place a link to your press kit and music. *Do not include attachments*! Ask them where you fit in and if you can also get a link on their web site or a featured section on their home page. Your "secret" promotional material page should make this job easier for them by providing a write-up, just in case they are too lazy to actually review your music. This may sound weird, but many ezines are starved for material and will be satisfied with your existing write-up or bio. This is another reason why it is paramount to review your press kit and convert it online.

Resources to Find Tons of Ezines

Ezine Directories

The Ultimate Band List
http://www.ubl.com/magazines.asp?mode=genre
Music Ezines from all over the world are listed by genre. A great place to start!

John Labovitz's Ezine List
http://www.meer.net/~johnl/e-zine-list
Comprehensive! Ordered by subject

Ezine Adsource
http://www.ezineadsource.com
Hundreds of ezines listed by category

Ezine Search Engines

Ezine Seek
http://www.ezineseek.com
Search for a music ezine that covers your genre.

Info Jump
http://www.infojump.com
Search through more than 5,000,000 electronic publication articles in 48 categories. Find and browse through 4,000 electronic publication titles.

News Resource
http://newo.com/news
Search for newspapers and magazines all over the world by region or keyword/subject.

World Press and Media Finder
http://www.escapeartist.com/media/media.htm
Categorized by Country.

Review Services

Another avenue you can explore are online review services. Each have different guidelines but they can provide a potential source of online traffic and exposure. The benefits of these services are that they link to your site and have a built-in audience looking for something new. You may not find your category or style is properly represented; but don't worry, many review services have a miscellaneous section. In addition, reviewer sites pop-up everyday and can be found with a search engine by querying on "CD review." Check out the most popular and long-standing online CD review services: **http://www.demorama.com** and **http://www.CDReviews.com** or to find more see *Internet Resources.*

These sites are easier to get reviews from than traditional print media, plus they have a link to your site for immediate reviewing of your songs or a download to listen to. This is something that traditional print media can't offer. Also, they are a great place to get your initial reviews, if you are starting out or if you don't have a write-up for your new hit song. The greatest thing about review services is that if you get a bad review, people can still decide for themselves by visiting your site.

Publishing Your Own Newsletter To Keep Fans Interested

Once you are getting some interest it is necessary to generate repeat traffic. Encourage visitors to "drop" you a line so they can be notified instantly of any new releases, gigs, upcoming events, changes to your site, etc. Being online enables you to do this instantaneously. (See *Using Email Effectively.*)

Building up an email list will bring in strong leads and is the most important ingredient to keeping interest in your music. In combination with an email list, a newsletter is the easiest way to generate repeat traffic. Make sure that your newsletter and site are updated constantly. Your newsletter doesn't have to be a twenty-page dynamo. It can be a short paragraph on your progress, interesting news about the band, touring stories, and URLs to new songs, releases, and photos. Be sure to include tour dates with city and state. You must be vigilant about keeping all information on your site fresh. Surfers have come to expect sites to be current. They will notice and come back to see what is new.

Thou Shalt Not Spam

Like any publication or broadcast media, send your press release with an appropriate cover letter. Most online publications prefer materials to be emailed. However, there are still some dinosaurs out there. A simple text message containing a cover letter, press release, and URL to your press kit will suffice. Whatever you do, *do not* send sound files, photos, or any other attachments to the recipient without permission. An editor will visit your site and review its contents if they feel your release is newsworthy. However, don't be shy. It is acceptable to ask them in the email if they would like an actual CD and press kit mailed to them and when and where.

Remember, not everyone runs the same operating system or email software. Attachments can get lost in translation and are an annoyance to editors. When mailing to several individuals, try to send every email to the person. If you can't or don't have time, be sure to use blind courtesy copy - especially for large lists! Avoiding these small oversights will give you an edge over many aspiring musicians that do not take the time to present themselves professionally. Otherwise, you will be mistaken for a Spammer. To give you an idea how easy it is to ruin your online reputation overnight, here's a story about abusing online publicity.

Another one of my clients was new to the Internet. They wanted to send a mass email to all of their contacts announcing their arrival on the web. I warned them about sending email to everyone without hiding the recipient list - blind courtesy copy (bcc:). They couldn't find the bcc: feature in their email program so they went ahead and sent out a message to some three hundred recipients. As a result, the recipients were visible to each other making my client's email list ripe for the picking. One of the recipients commandeered the list and emailed everyone back announcing an up coming event with an attached graphic file, which boasted his scorching guitar and vocals. I sent a friendly email to both my client and the offender pointing out that what he did is considered "spamming," not to mention that some of the individuals on the list were A&R reps! He claimed that he was new to email and didn't know any better.

After my client had worked so hard to build a strong email list, he threw it away with the click of a button. Make sure before you email to more than one person, that you blind courtesy copy (bcc:) every one!

TIME TO CHECK IN:

• Make Sure Your Online Press Kit is Ready for Prime Time

❏ Double Check Your Materials

Make sure that your site communicates clearly how to contact you and where to go get more info for write-ups. In the event you are contacted by editors or program managers, always be professional and prompt in your replies!

• Draft An Email "Cover Letter" For Contacting Station Managers

❏ Keep Your Correspondence Professional and to the Point

Avoid a "desperate" tone of voice in your letter. You want to come across as a confident veteran of the industry. Don't forget to include the URL for your online press kit.

• Draft Newsletter For Potential Exposure Gained

❏ Include News, Discounts on Merchandise and CD, & Events Calendar

When the publicity flood gates start to open, your new fans will want to know everything about your latest ventures. Having a newsletter ready to roll will save you the headache of growing pains and show that you are a true professional.

• Get Your CD Reviewed

❏ Submit Your CD to the more reputable Review Sites

www.demorama.com, www.cdreviews.com, www.indiepromo.com/reviewers

❏ Find Ezines to Review Your CD and Write-up Your Act/Site

Visit UBL and BandUtopia to find publications that cover your genre(s). Don't forget local music scene sites in your "sphere of influence" and in areas that you tour. Also, be sure to refer to the Ezine resources table in *Internet Radio & Online Publicity: Ezines*.

❑ Contact Every Applicable Ezine You Find

Remember, approach Ezines like you would any other high-profile media. Unless a publication expressly permits it, do not send any pictures, songs, or press materials with out their permission first.

• Begin Penetrating Internet Radio Based On Success with Reviews

❑ Find Reputable Internet Radio Stations

Visit the MIT Radio Directory, the Online Radio Directory, and IndiePromo.com's list of stations looking for submissions. Before submitting any material, be sure that the station is:

1. Licensed with your Performance Right Organization.
2. Has you sign a distribution agreement, not all of your rights away.
3. Has DJ's or a Programming manager so you can forge a relationship.

❑ Contact Appropriate Sites

Describe your music and include your URL to your press kit page. If you are a crossover artist, ask where you fit into their programming. You may get several songs on different programs!

• Integrate Your Site With Any Exposure Gained

❑ Place Write-Ups from Reviewers & Ezines in Your Newsletter & Site

Don't forget to link back to the site or publication that reviewed you!

❑ Link to Radio Stations That Are Giving You Airplay

Don't forget:

1. D.J. or Station Manager email links for requests.
2. Broadcast range and Station ID (freq. and call letters) for offline stations.
3. URL to Page on Internet station where your hit song can be heard.

NOTES:

NOTES:

CHAPTER 14

Covering Your Bases

So far we have only covered a small portion of promoting your web site online and where most of your focus should be applied. When you have addressed or even exhausted all of the resources discussed in previous chapters, begin to concentrate on the rest of the traditional means of promoting web sites online. They are newsgroups, discussion groups, web rings, music site awards, and banner ads.

The methods covered in this chapter are what most of the "small guy's" are doing online to promote their site and can involve a lot more work for a lot less return if handled poorly. However, I will show you how to use these old methods more effectively and how to stand out as a true professional among the other "small bean" web sites. Let's begin with exploring newsgroups.

How to Use Newsgroups Effectively

Newsgroups are a vast and incredibly varied collection of *virtual* bulletin boards where individuals can post messages for others to read and respond to. There are literally tens of thousands of groups pulsating with correspondence worldwide on the Internet. Topics cover everything imaginable from the informative, to the tasteless, to the morbid, to the ridiculous - and believe it or not, music, too. In this section, we will briefly explore how newsgroups and discussion groups can help you; where to find them; when it is appropriate to use them; and how to identify appropriate ones for posting announcements.

Searching for Groups That Are Useful

Finding a useful newsgroup can appear to be daunting a task. There are more than 30,000 groups on the Internet and tens of thousands more that have a limited distribution. On top of that, Online Services (AOL, CompuServe and Microsoft Network) and search engines have thousands of their own. Fortunately, you don't have to read through all of them to find your topic of interest.

The first place to begin is by using the newsgroup program built in to your web browser or email reader. With a connection to your local ISP news server, you can grab a list of all the newsgroups that it has available and search for an appropriate subject by keyword. Unfortunately, most ISP's subscribe to a tiny fraction of available newsgroups. So if the subject you are interested in isn't on your ISP's list, you can ask them to subscribe to it if you know the exact name of the group.

Some towns and municipalities have newsgroups for announcing local events, personal comments and entertainment reviews, places to hang out, etc. These *local* newsgroups can be used to announce gigs, anything new that happens to your career, or to post news releases. You only have access to them if you use a local ISP to connect to the Internet. This is why I encouraged you to have separate ISP from a Web Host Provider in *Online Basics & Putting Your Music Online*.

> Visit Newbie-U on how to setup your newsgroup program. Internet Explorer and Netscape Communicator come with one built in.
>
> http://www.newbie-u.com

Public Access News Servers

If your ISP doesn't provide news servers, you can use other means to gain access and search for newsgroups with *public news servers*. One of the best ways to locate useful newsgroups is at the DejaNews web site - http://www.dejanews.com. It's operates like a search engine and let's you search by keyword or subject.

Public Access Newsgroup Servers

DejaNews – http://www.dejanews.com
Free access to 80,000 newsgroups and discussion groups.

RemarQ – http://www.remarq.com
Free access to 30,000 newsgroups through their web site, or $12 a month to use your newsreader

**Yahoo! – http://dir.yahoo.com/Computers_and_Internet/Internet/Usenet/
Public_Access_Usenet_Sites**
Comprehensive directory of public news servers

You can also access newsgroups with regular search engines. Infoseek has one of the best interfaces available and a powerful search feature - http://www.infoseek.com. See the table on the previous page to find more public news servers and information on newsgroups.

It's All Subjective: Newsgroup Categories

There are so many ideas expressed in newsgroups, that without any type of naming scheme, it would be impossible to find any useful newsgroups to promote your site. Although newsgroups come in different varieties on the Internet and Online Services, I will limit this discussion to the naming scheme that most newsgroups are based upon.

Newsgroup names start with a category, followed by a period, then a subject which can be followed by a number of subcategories, each separated by another dot. For example, *alt.music.songwriter* is a group in the major category of "alternative" that allows songwriters to talk about anything pertaining to their craft. It is pronounced "alt dot music dot songwriters" and is affectionately called AMS by regulars. Abbreviating a newsgroup name is common practice of experienced *newsgroupies*. Not all newsgroups on songwriting and music are in the ALT category. Many reside in "recreation" (REC) such as *rec.musicmakers*. Below is a table on *Newsgroup Categories* for their definitions and the various ways you can promote your web site in them.

Newsgroup Categories

ALT

Alternative covers topics that are considered "offbeat" and outside of normal daily conversation. Even road-kill pictures are things that can be found here. There is a gold mine of music topics here, as well. However, many of them are merely fan gossip and idolization of commercial acts. If your music sounds like one of these acts, present your music in that light – i.e. "If you like the Eagles' *Hotel California* then you will like the sounds of …"

BIZ

Business related - Postings containing advertising and promotion. Some are truthful, most are straight out of infomercial scripts. Commercial announcements are welcomed here even though frowned upon in other categories. You could finagle your way into some groups in this category, if you write music for corporate productions, conventions, etc.

COMP

Anything related to computers. This one is hard to penetrate but you will find some useful software for your craft in this category.

NEWS

Dealing with Usenet itself (the people who brought you newsgroups), including administration, announcements and new groups. You should announce your arrival on the web or any major revamps to your site here, i.e. *news.announce.newsites*, etc.

REC

Recreation is the theme here, anything from basket weaving to science fiction paraphernalia, from pets to sports, to whatever you can think of. An incredible amount of music topics here - rec.musicmakers and rec.musicmakers.<your-instrument-here>.

SCI

The wonderful world of science and logic. Unless your music is about Protons stay clear of this category. Geeks are a very dangerous lot and were the first ones to "live" on the Internet. They also know how to "attack" Spammers and have the time on their hands to do so.

SOC

Short for "social." This category deals with social and cultural issues. If you write songs about social issues, you could promote your site in this category. Tread lightly, though. Some of the topics can be a sensitive spot for readers.

TALK

This is where to find controversial subjects, such as abortion and gun control. Penetrate this category in the same way described in SOC.

MISC

Miscellaneous is the place for anything that doesn't really fit anywhere else. This category is a mess. Your posts will most likely go unnoticed but it probably wouldn't hurt to dig around for a topic of interest.

There is helpful information available for those that don't know what topic to look for in newsgroups. Comprehensive lists of newsgroup categories can be found with the following online resources:

```
┌─────────────────────────────────────────────────────────────────┐
│                                                                 │
│              Places to Find More Newsgroups                     │
│                                                                 │
│   Internet FAQ Consortuim – http://www.faqs.org                 │
│   Liszt – http://www.liszt.com/news                             │
│   Tile.Net – http://www.tile.net/news                           │
│   Usenet Info Center – http://metalab.unc.edu/usenet-i          │
│   Yahoo! Newsgroup Listings –                                   │
│   http://dir.yahoo.com/Computers_and_Internet/Internet/Usenet/Newsgroup_Listings │
│                                                                 │
└─────────────────────────────────────────────────────────────────┘
```

Now that you know how to find worthy newsgroups, let's take a moment to talk about online etiquette and how to stay out of trouble.

Coming Out of Hiding: Lurking & Delurking

Before posting to *any* newsgroup or discussion list, follow some of the *threads* to see what is considered fair game. Threads are replies to a single post – a discussion on one topic. You will be able to tell right off the bat if a newsgroup is the right topic and if groupies are open to commercial announcements. This is known as *lurking*. When you are ready to make your presence known, *delurk* yourself and post a useful message.

The Flood is Coming: Why Lurking Works

Many newsgroups have FAQ's (Frequently Asked Questions documents) or charters than explain the purpose of the group and what kinds of messages are acceptable. In *moderated* or monitored newsgroups, reading the FAQ is extremely important. If you post something considered inappropriate, the moderator won't allow your message to appear on the group and may send you a nasty note. Some groups that are moderated may place a signature at the bottom of every post explaining where to find the FAQ and others automatically post the full text on a regular basis.

If you *flood* every music newsgroup on the Internet without *delurking* first, you are abusing an already overloaded resource. Moderated groups will ignore your message and groupies in unmediated ones will get ticked off, causing them to *flame* you. Flaming is when a *newsgroupie* will try to publicly humiliate a reckless Poster by replying to the offending post and flooding the Poster with emails that announce how clueless he is.

Newsgroupies have every reason to get upset because there are forums reserved for announcements. There have been instances where reckless posters found newsletters, emails, and other various sorted types of announcements filling up their mailboxes that they didn't subscribe to. They were *mail bombed* by the best of the best online. Again, the only sure fired way to avoid getting shunned online is to lurk around newsgroups you are interested in, to get the lay of the land.

How Newsgroups Should Be Used for Exposure

Before I get into any details, understand that *newsgroups are not well suited for marketing your music or plugging your CD.* However, *newsgroups are useful for promoting your web site.* This is because blatant commercialism is frowned down upon and has seriously degraded the effectiveness of newsgroups. Again, before unleashing a mass broadcast, make sure it is okay to post an announcement by *lurking* around in the newsgroups you are interested in.

Admittedly, it is easy to abuse newsgroups because they appear to be unmonitored. This is not necessarily true. There can be a group of individuals in any given newsgroup enforcing *netiquette,* an unwritten law regarding Internet behavior. In some cases, you will have to be creative and reply to a posting, answer a question, or solve someone's problem while slipping in that you have a new site, etc. Keep in mind, your signature will be slipping in a blurb about your site, while you do this.

How to Get Ignored in Newsgroups

Your access to newsgroups comes with great responsibility. Now that you have the power to reach hundreds, even thousands of people with the click of a button, it is extremely important to think about what you are going to say and how to say it. The trick is to get people interested in your site without them being aware they are receiving a sales pitch. Let me show you what I mean.

Too often when I am reading newsgroups, I see posts like this:

```
New MP3 site.  Check this cool site out.
http://members.aol.com/cybersnoogie
```

Even worse, a post in all capitals:

```
CHECK THIS SITE OUT!
WE ARE THE BEST HEAVY METAL BAND!
VISIT US NOW OR BE SUBJUGATED TO EXTREME PAIN!
HTTP://WWW.UNKOWNISP.COM/METALROCKS
```

All I have to say is *nobody cares*! Why should anyone visit these sites? Announcements like these are considered obnoxious by groupies and look similar to thousands of other posts. So what is missing? Obvious benefits to readers. Sure, some people will visit as a result of these posts, but not enough to make it worth scouring through endless newsgroups for your topic of interest and then posting an uninteresting message.

Be A Giver, Not A Taker

Your message has to communicate overly obvious benefits that make readers hungry to visit your site. Post a message that gives people something to walk away with:

```
Enter to win a free CD and receive a free T-shirt or sticker of
your choice.  Visit the Ralph Mongers web site now: http://
www.ralphmongers.com.  Punk that will make you puke!
```

Notice there is no screaming in capital letters and the benefit of getting something for free. The commercial intent of this post is less obvious and the purpose for visiting their site is clear. Ads of this nature are usually acceptable and yield minimum complaints. Another method is to "talk" to a newsgroup or ask for help:

```
Hi, I've just started a Punk band called the Ralph Mongers.  We
are looking for some good venues to perform in and online
resources to help us get the word out.  Visit us at http://
www.ralphmongers.com.
```

You could instead say, "we have set up a web site with Punk music promotion resources and are looking for more." Either way, you haven't posted an "ad" and you appear as a real person. Not only that, you may get some more resources to help you spread the word. Again, make sure that your posts provide useful information or offer something for free. Avoid posting commercial announcements. Benefits, benefits, benefits!

More Newsgroup Pitfalls

In addition to drab postings, there are more newsgroup follies to avoid.

- **Do not post tour dates.** They are absolutely of no interest to the majority of readers outside of your geographical area. However, it is acceptable to post dates on local area newsgroups and discussion groups. Use DejaNews to search for newsgroups for the areas you gig in.

- **Do not directly promote your CD or music.** Only promote your web site. The whole idea is to drive people to your site so that you can get their contact information and keep drilling them for a sale.

- **Do not post to unrelated newsgroups.** For example, posting your "new music site" announcement on *alt.embroidery* will bring you some heat. This is considered spamming and can have adverse affects to your online "well being." However, if one of your songs is about the *pleasure of quilting*, you have a unique opportunity to gain some exposure.

- **Avoid** *cross posting* or sending your post to more than several newsgroups at a time. Some news servers watch out for this and will kill your message, causing it to have a severely limited distribution.

- **Avoid Frequent Posts.** Some news servers also watch out for the same message being frequently posted and will kill it. You could also get banned by a moderator for this kind of activity.

- **Avoid attaching pictures and sounds to posts.** Don't give away stuff on newsgroups. Encourage surfers to visit your site to acquire the "good stuff" with a benefit-rich message.

- **Create a Signature.** Even if you are responding to posts unrelated to promoting your site – i.e. asking about a MIDI software program on *alt.music.software* – your site will get a small plug at the end of your posts. Most web browsers, that are email capable, use your email signature file. See *Signatures* in *Using Email Effectively*, to learn how to write an effective signature.

How Often Should I Post?

Depending on how active a group is, you may find a huge jump in traffic on your site for a couple of days. The best way to test results is by releasing announcements in groups of similar interest. This will isolate whether or not your release has an impact or that the subject is not of interest to anyone. If you get poor results, rewrite it and try again a few days later.

Mail Lists & Email Discussion Groups

Mail lists are discussion groups based on the email system. The good thing about them is that they tend to be more close-knit. The bad thing is that they get off the topic rather easily. Mailling Lists can also be especially annoying since every time somebody sends a message to the group it arrives in your mailbox. (Remember those lame posts earlier?) However, one can get around this. Some mail lists are sophisticated enough to hold every message sent in an archive until the end of the day. This is called a *digest* and is much more manageable.

Mail List Etiquette

The same rule of thumb for newsgroups applies to mail lists. If there is an archive web site for the mail list you are interested in, you will be able to read the charter and lurk around a bit without having to subscribe. Do not ignore the charter. Mail list groupies are notoriously impatient with new posters. Word your promotional emails so that they are giving advice or free tips and let your signature do the promoting.

If you do not prepare a carefully written email, you may have to change your address for all of your trouble. Be prepared to get *spammed* back with negative responses if you post a commercial message. See *Internet Resources* or visit **http://IndiePromo.com** for some informative mailing lists. To find more music related lists on your own visit: **http://www.lizst.com**. For now, the table on the next page will get you off to a good start.

Swapping Links 101

Search engines are not always the start of a surfer's search for the ultimate web site. Many times a surfer happens upon a link within a relevant Web page or directory, which you can acquire with a simple request. By providing "free stuff," you can easily finagle your way onto a web masters "useful" or "free" links page within a larger site. Web masters like to link other sites that make theirs look good. Always approach web masters with some flattery. If you can, try to find out their name and investigate the site before making first contact but don't come on too strong. By doing some research, you can make compliments on various parts of a master's page. Doing this will grab their attention and warm them up to you immediately because you show knowledge and interest in their site. Then, mention you have given them a link on your site - after doing it of course. Finally, mention what your site has to offer. Since you have gained intimate

Some Great Places to Find Discussion Lists

OneList – http://www.onelist.com
Searchable list of discussion lists. Try searching on "indie music" or "music promotion"

EGroups – http://www.egroups.com
More discussion lists you can search on.

Topica – http://www.topica.com
Search here too.

Publicly Accessible Mailing Lists – http://www.neosoft.com/internet/paml

Non-Commerical Resources

ListServ - http://scout.cs.wisc.edu
Announcements for New Lists and an Archive

New-List - http://www.new-list.com
Have email announcements sent to you whenever a new music related list is started.

Tile.Net – http://tile.net/lists
For some of you old school hackers – Lyris, majordomo, and listproc *lists*

Vivian Neou's List of Lists – http://catalog.com/vivian

Liszt – http://www.liszt.com
A Huge list of discussion groups

You can also search Yahoo! on "mailing list" and "discussion group"

knowledge of a web master's site, you know what is of interest to his/her visitors. Web masters love adoration. They are the unsung heroes of the popular-information age. However, keep your request short - 3 to 4 sentences. *Do not* approach them with *Please visit my Web site at http://www.here.com. If you link to me, I'll give you a link back.* Requests of this nature are typically ignored.

Who To Ask

A quick way to find potential "link swappers" is to search on one of your keywords. Visit the top listings and ask the web master to swap links as outlined previously. These sites are the busiest and may swap links with you. Then again, they may be arrogant because they are on top...tread lightly! Remember, you must have something of value or you are wasting both their time and yours.

Who Not To Ask

Try to avoid sites like "Uncle Joey's Page of Links." These tend to be disorganized and poorly maintained. It is better not to associate your site with them. All of your links should enhance your appearance, not detract from it. Linking to a low quality site makes yours low quality. Once your professional façade is broken, visitors won't come back or recommend your site to others.

SWAP TIPS

Stay On the Topic: Links to and from your site should be music related. For example, if you have written a song about a specific subject, i.e. saving the whales, try to negotiate reciprocal links to sites that have an interest in that subject.

Quality, not Quantity: After going through all the trouble of getting a professional looking site, you don't want a tacky McDonald's color-schemed gun silencer outlet linked to your site. Don't go for numbers! Go for high quality and useful links.

Web Rings

With so much media attention on the Internet in just the past few years, the World Wide Web has gone through several popularity explosions. As a result, there are so many web sites unleashed daily that it can take several weeks before a Web page is listed in a search engine. One of our clients reported that he was not listed on Yahoo until four months after his site was "suggested." As you know now, this fellow was actually extremely fortunate. Undoubtedly, search engines are on the verge of becoming tapped out. Surfers enter a small request and receive thousands of *hits*, making it almost impossible for your site to be ranked anywhere near the top. (See *Improving Your Rankings* in *Understanding Search Engines.*) Fortunately there are other resources available where a site can target more surfers within a *specific interest* group. One is the Web Ring.

How Web Rings Work

When a site joins a ring, web "neighbors" reside to the left and right. A surfer that keeps going to the left will eventually end up where he/she started. A site can belong to several rings, enhancing the possibility of more traffic.

Web Rings are numerous and FREE. Every ring on the Internet is listed at the Web Ring Directory - **http://www.webring.org**. There you can search a comprehensive index for a ring that suits your niche. There are hundreds of music related rings that cover topics that include: genres, industry and professional, commercial band idolatry, instruments, songwriters, gender, etc. All contain multiple sites that could bring in more traffic to your web site.

What to Watch Out For

Ring Masters rarely deny membership as they are trying to increase traffic to their site. If you can't find a web ring to suit your musical style, then you can create your own and become a Ring Master. Still, it is best to keep the number of rings you join limited to three. Anymore is considered tacky and will lag your site's load time. Also, try to join rings with less than 300 sites. Large rings tend to generate less traffic because they are more likely to be "broken." Again, keep in mind that since Ring Masters are not denying other artists request to join, you may get your site "ringed" with a large number of artists you don't like or you feel are substantially far behind your musical stage. Carefully review the rings you are considering joining.

http://www.webring.org

Web Site Awards

Submitting your site for an award is a good way to direct some highly targeted traffic to your site for a few days. There are literally thousands of awards to choose from. The only problem is which ones are the best for getting your site exposure? Apply to well-known awards first and then work your way down the totem pole. It is best to go for music site awards - genre, industry, instruments, etc. - because the traffic that could be generated is highly targeted.

If you do get an award, your traffic will increase for a short while. Consider this option only if you have spare time on your hands or have exhausted all of your leads. Otherwise it is not worth your effort. See the table below for a list of sites that rate awards and categorize them by interest.

The More Reputable Award Sites

Project Cool - http://www.projectcool.com/sightings/
The Original since 1994

USA Today Hot Site - http://www.usatoday.com/life/cyber/ch.htm
USA Today elects five hot sites every weekday except Fridays.

Yahoo! What's New - http://www.yahoo.com/picks
If your site is picked, you will get an entry into their search engine, huge mention in the Yahoo! What's New, and a cool little pair of sunglasses next to your site.

NetGuide Internet Site of the Day - http://www.netguide.com
NetGuide has various categories to submit to. Visit their site to find the appropriate one and look for an email link to send in your submission.

Sites That Track Lesser Known Awards

Award Sites! – http://www.awardsites.com
Lists 900 awards and rates them from 1 to 5.

Web Site Awards – http://websiteawards.xe.net
Lists over 800 awards and helps you track your progress.

Search on "music web site awards" in your favorite search engine.

An Argument Against Using Awards

Many gurus recommend that you submit your site to every "cool site" award you can find. Be extremely careful. *Some sites are fronts for email clearing houses.* Award sites have been known to sell the email addresses they gather to salesmen and spammers. I haven't found evidence to support this rumor, but it could be possible for someone to start an award for that purpose.

Banner Mania

Banner ads are those animated advertisements plastered all over a web site. You may have considered using them to get more online exposure. At first glance, they seem like a great way to generate traffic to your site. However, they can end up burning a big hole in your pocket with little or no results. Only the pros seem to be able to afford a real banner ad campaign. Even though there are free "trading networks" that allow you to distribute your own personal banner ads, the basic principle here is that you get what you pay for.

FREE Banner Exchanges?!

Free banner exchanges are an entirely different animal from paid banner advertising. Paid banners are highly targeted and will generate more sales for you, unlike the numerous banner exchange programs lurking on the World Wide Web touting free FREE FREE!!! *Free systems will do you little or no good for you and can even cause harm.* Here are two scenarios:

Scenario A: A surfer is browsing a site on the subject of game software. He sees your eye catching banner and clicks on it. Great...right? The problem is that your page is a music site. The surfer is then dissatisfied because he is not interested in music. He was most likely curious about your banner and clicked on impulse. Still, his mind is on games and you are selling music. You are not likely to get even an email address out of him. As simplified as this example is, it only focuses on the other web page - where your banner was displayed. But what if a banner on your site loaded as "Bestiality Chat Room?"

Lesson A: With banner exchanges, you have little control over the quality and content of banners popping up on your site and other web pages that display your banner.

Scenario B: You spent days, maybe months of hard work on your site to make it just right to get a listing on Yahoo! Finally, you get listed and a lot of hits start to generate traffic to your site. Voila! Visitors from Yahoo! and the first thing you do is guide them to another web page with a banner on your site that promises "All Healing Prune Juice." They just can't pass this up and leave your site without hearing your music!

Lesson B: Once you have captivated a surfer why encourage them to leave? If you are itching to try banners place them deep within your site.

How Banner Systems Work & The Problems They Cause

When a site is getting next to no traffic or starting out, there are even more reasons to avoid banner exchanges. To see what I mean it is necessary to understand how banner exchanges work.

Earning Credit Where Credit Is Due

Each banner exchange has a different *credit* system. The most common are ratio based. Ratio based banner exchanges are gauged by impressions - the number of times a banner is displayed. For example, a 1/2 ratio will get you one impression - on another Web page - for every two impressions of another site's banner within your page. This is a very generous 50% return. These days you will find more common ratios of 9/10 (90%) or 4/5 (80%). These may look extremely enticing but with a 9/10 ratio you will have to display someone else's banner ten times before you get nine impressions elsewhere. This is horrible for the individual musician site starting out. Still, after all of the trouble both sites went through to build up nine credits, surfers may never click on any of the banners displayed! Again keep in mind that your music ad could be showing up right now on a site promoting a senior citizen community.

Many banner services are now using a rating system based on the amount of traffic you already receive. For example, if you receive 500 visitors on a page that displays a banner your rating is category B. If you receive 1000 hits you're granted category A. Category B will get you 100 impressions on various sites and A gets you 250. While you are building 500 hits, no one has seen your banner. To add insult to injury, when you finally accumulate enough hits, you can not select or have any control over the sites your banner appears on. What if your banner ad appeared a number of times in the

Animal Sex Chat room! As you can see, no one is doing you any favors. You will still have to build traffic through conventional means - search engines, newsgroups, press releases, link swapping, etc.

Paid Banner Campaigns - You Get What You Pay For

If you have the money, paid banners can benefit you in many ways. Some sites charge by click-through - how many times your banner will be "clicked on." Most charge per thousand impressions (CPM). This is the number of times your banner ad is displayed. In order to get the best possible results, you will have to invest more money into a banner that screams CLICK ME! Banner design is a science of its own. Not every web designer is adept at it.

Targeted Audiences

The major advantage to paid banner advertising is that you choose the page where your banner will appear. This freedom of choice allows you to place your banner on a topic that suits your niche. This guarantees that the surfer clicking through to your page is already interested in what your site has to offer. There are also keywords for sale on every major search engine. For example, if you buy the keyword "singer," your banner and site will be displayed - first - every time a surfer searches on "singer." (Information *is* power...scary isn't it?) Cost is determined by the popularity of the keyword. So don't choose "sex" - you can't afford it.

The Church of Yahoo!

Once again, Yahoo! has broken the mold and done their own thing. They avoid all of this mess and confusion by selling blocks of time. In their great wisdom, Yahoo! views the web as television and treats their advertising as such. You can get some big exposure for just a hundred dollars. Visit Yahoo! and click on advertising on the bottom of their home page for more information: http://www.yahoo.com.

Where is the Best Place to Put a Banner on My Site?

There has been a lot of research and speculation on banner placement. Many agree that placing a graphic banner in the lower right hand corner of the first screenful is best. (by the scrollbar and where the mouse is used the most in a web browser's window.) This location is said to generate as high as a 228% higher click-through rate than banners at the top of a page. Other studies show that banners placed a third down a page yield up to 77% click-through rates. Nonetheless, banner placement is as much an art as it is science.

Setting Up an Affiliate: An Alternate to Banner Exchanges

Another way to get more traffic to your site is to give out a small graphic banner with your logo. Encourage fans to put this graphic on their page and link to your site. A good incentive is a contest for free music or tickets. To implement this campaign, you will need to set up a "linking information" page that shows surfers how to link to you. This will make it quick and easy for any interested parties. On that page offer a text link, a graphic or small banner link, and if you are feeling spunky, a button link. Show the code on how to set up each. This will take some HTML knowhow or you can always enlist the help of an "old web salt." The downside to linking "made easy" for your visitors is that you have no control over the quality of sites that link to you. If this is a major concern, then *moderate* - take a peak - before swapping links with fans and other music related sites.

TIME TO CHECK IN:

- ## Generate More Traffic To Your Site

  - ❑ ### Create A Signature File If You Haven't Yet
    With a signature file configured in your email and newsgroup programs, every post and email you send will have your essential contact information - email, URL, and Band Name.

  - ❑ ### Draft Your Announcement
    Keep it short and to the point. Word it so that visitors will know why they should visit your site. Just try to pique interest; don't give the hard sell. Try offering something free or have a contest of some sort.

  - ❑ ### Find Applicable Newsgroups To Promote Your Site
    If you can't find any decent groups through your local ISP, use DejaNews to do a search and post your announcements. Remember, newsgroups are not a good place to promote your CD! Only use them to promote your site! Follow the examples on how to draft your message.

  - ❑ ### Find Applicable Email Lists
    Look at the table of resources for a starting point.

  - ❑ ### Grow Your Own Email List
    Try to make giving an email address the easiest and quickest thing visitors can do on your site. Having a clickable button that automatically sends you an email address is the simplest solution.

- ## Generate Online Awareness

  - ❑ ### Ask Web Masters For Tips
    Visit your favorite web site and ask their web masters for tips. Web masters love adoration.

  - ❑ ### Start Researching Web Rings
    Find the best Web Ring that suits your site, i.e. specific genres, interest, instruments, etc. Visit www.webring.org to search their index.

❑ Awards

See the table on Award resources to find an appropriate award for your site. Try to shoot for high-profile awards and then work your way down the "totem pole" to the lesser known awards.

❑ Find Other Sites to Swap Links

Swap only with professional looking sites. Stay on the topic of music. Create a "how to" page for fans to increase the incentive.

❑ Consider Banners As A Last Resort

Avoid using other banners on your site if at all possible - i.e. only distribute yours. Banners only do a site good if there is already a lot of traffic. Before you consider using them, grow you traffic by traditional means - i.e. search engines, announcements, email, etc. If you join a banner exchange program, place any banners deep within your site - i.e. sub-pages like your guest book, after an order has been submitted, etc.

NOTES:

NOTES:

CHAPTER 15

Measuring Your Success

Now that you've unleashed your propaganda machine onto the world, you need to track its results. The Internet is an extremely useful tool for this. From using search engines to paying thousands of dollars for professional clipping services, you can literally hear what your buzz sounds like.

What Does Your Buzz Sound Like?

Using Search Engines to Monitor Your Exposure

Seeing if your band name appears online is easy. All you have to do is search on it. If your name is too generic or relates to a popular subject matter, place some music related keywords into your search. For example, "ralph mongers MP3" or in place of "MP3," try "music" or "band," or the region where you perform or your genre. This should narrow things down significantly.

Perform a search on the Big Seven and a few Meta-Search sites to get a cursory view. You may find some useful tie-ins to exposing your music. Results can be unpredictable. Don't spend too much of your time poking around on search engines if your results are not telling you anything.

There are many more useful methods for tracking your online exposure, including free automated search services. Some allow you to track keywords in specific search engines, while others can watch specific web pages for updates. See the table on the next page for their locations.

Peacefire offers a free service called, TrackerLock that allows you to monitor Alta Vista with five sets of keywords. For example, you could track your group's online "foot print" with all of the following:

"ralph mongers"
punk AND "ralph mongers"

"los angeles" AND punk AND MP3
"punk rock" AND MP3
"underground punk"

Notice all of the keywords are in lowercase. Alta Vista is not case sensitive, but if you enter all of your keywords in lowercase, it will find, Punk Rock, punk rock, Punk rock, etc. Where as entering "Punk Rock" will only yield instances of "Punk Rock."

When a match is found, the first ten will be sent to you in an email. Even though TrackerLock only searches AltaVista, you can get a pretty good idea of where you stand with your keywords and will most certainly find any mention of you online.

The Informant is another useful free service that covers a lot more ground. After registering with them, you can monitor up to three queries. As with TrackerLock, you can tell it how often you want the search to be performed, anywhere between three to sixty day intervals. Plus you can have it search on any one of the following search engines: Alta Vista, Excite, Lycos, or InfoSeek.

In addition, The Informant will let you watch up to five URLs for any changes. When the specified amount of time has past, the search is performed and any monitored URLs are checked for changes. The top ten results and any URL changes are then sent to your mailbox.

Watching URLs allows you to monitor your search engine ranking. All you have to do is paste that long ugly web address you get, after clicking the search button, into The Informant. It will look something like this:

```
http://www.altavista.com/cgi-bin/query?=pg=q&kl=XX&q=punk+rock
```

Resources to Help You Track Your Online Footprint

TrackerLock – http://www.peacefire.org/tracerlock
The Informant – http://informant.dartmouth.edu/
URL-Minder – http://www.netmind.com/html/url-minder.html

If five URLs are not enough for your needs, there is another free service called, URL-Minder. This kick ass service will allow you to enter as many URLs as you want. So now, you can watch your search engine ranking on all of the search engines for free. However, you get what you pay for. URL-Minder seems to have a mind of its own. It sends you the first page of results periodically and isn't as reliable as TracerLock. But the advantage is that you can monitor more resources in one place.

Places to Find Buzz About You in Newsgroups

DejaNews – http://www.dejanews.com
remarQ – http://www.remarq.com

What Do People Say About You in Newsgroups?

You can search a large number of newsgroups by using **DejaNews** and **remarQ**. DejaNews has the most advanced search capability and access to 80,000 newsgroups and forums. It should be the first place to check for any gossip about you. RemarQ has a fairly limited search feature that only accepts keywords or phrases. Still, they archive 30,000 newsgroups. It's free...use it.

Clipping Services

If you have the money, online clipping services can cover a lot more ground for you. One of note uses both automated searches and human scouring. It is affectionately called, CyberAlert – **http://www.cyberalert.com**. They pretty much have the Web covered. For a fee, they compose information daily by scouring for topics of interest to you in general search engines, forums, specialty search engines, and online databases.

At the end of the day, you can login to their web site and grab the results. This service starts at $1,995 a month. If you are interested in monitoring offline publications, search Yahoo! on "monitoring and clipping services." The are many services available in a wide range of cost. However, be forewarned. Offline clipping services are notoriously limited when it comes to niche markets like music.

How to Check Offline Publications On Your Own

Several search engines have the capability to track news in the offline world. The leaders are Excite and Northern Light. See the table below for more handy free offline clipping services.

Free Tools Available for Searching Offline Publications

Excite's News Tracker – http://nt.excite.com
Norhtern Light – http://www.northerlight.com/news.html

Places to Search Archives

Hot Bot: News Channel – http://www.newsbot.com
Newshub – http://www.newshub.com
TotalNEWS – http://www.totalnews.com

News Hunt – http://www.newshunt.com
Contains links to newspaper and other publication archives

Other Stuff Under Your Nose

Part of a successful marketing campaign is knowing which methods of promotion or advertising are most effective. Your web site will make this an effortless task by tracking visitor activity automatically in "access" logs. In this section, I will show you different methods of making use of them. Note that not all web host providers offer this service. So before signing up for web space, make sure that access logs are included as part of your service agreement - standalone Web Host Providers are more likely to come with this capability as a standard feature. Although you can use free access tracking services, they detract from your professional façade and slow your site.

User Profile by Regions

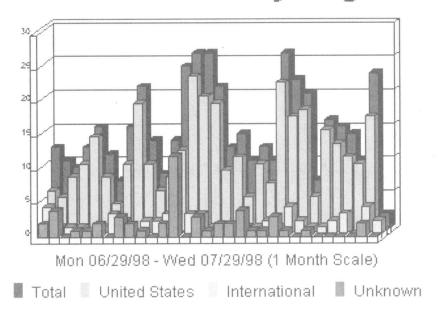

Mon 06/29/98 - Wed 07/29/98 (1 Month Scale)

■ Total ■ United States ■ International ■ Unknown

Statistic Programs

Statistic programs read a site's access log and graph this information in a useful format for you to see. With such programs, you can monitor which pages are accessed the most and which are accessed the least. Web statistic software also gives you an idea of what is happening in a web site by showing what countries visitors arrive from, the most commonly clicked songs, which pages surfers are reading the most, the average length of time a visitor stays, and more.

With all of this information, you can "fine tune" your web site on the fly, not to mention hone your marketing skills and help shape your overall strategy. A good web master makes this a full time effort. Ask yours what he/she charges to do this. Statistic software is for the more web savvy but if you must know how many people visit your site and you don't want a whole lot of detailed information, then *access counters* can give you a rough idea. If your web provider doesn't offer utilities to track site access, check out Link Exchange to obtain a free access counter: **http://www.linkexchange.com**

or go to your favorite search engine and query on "free access counter." Keep in mind that you get what you pay for. These so-called "free services" can slow down your web page, too.

Back Link Checking

An extremely useful method in tracking your promotion efforts is Back Link Checking. This is one of the first things I do when I get up in the morning to work on my promotional material. Simply put, all you have to do is open up your access log software and look for any domain names of web sites that you either submitted material to or requested to be reviewed. You can also see what keywords are being used to find you in search engines!

Page Access

With most access log software, you can also check which pages are being accessed the most and how long. If you find that the average visit to your music page is under a minute, then something there is turning off visitors. Not necessarily your music, but maybe your page is difficult to navigate. Even worse, your site isn't providing a link to the software required to listen to your music and visitors are too lazy to open up another browser window to get it. Maybe they don't know where to begin or your content is not grabbing their attention. The point is that you can find flaws in your site design and content that could deter most visitors from coming back or exploring further. Even worse, visitors with a sour taste in their mouth from your site, could lead to their telling others how horrible your site is.

I can tell you from personal experience that I improved my readership drastically in my second year of operation by just placing a "subscribe here" message at the top of every page on my site. I discovered this when I took my daily look at the access logs and found that I had increased my traffic over time, but the rate of new subscribers didn't. I suddenly realized that only two pages on my site had the ability to add subscribers to my newsletter. Doah! The same method should be used for your CD. Every page on your site should, in effect, funnel visitors to your order page or subscription list.

TIME TO CHECK IN:

· Monitor Search Engines

❑ Check Your Keywords' Effectiveness

Use TrackerLock and the other services outlined in *Measuring Your Success*.

❑ Check Newsgroups for Buzz About You

Use DejaNews to search on your name or band, or to find any potential resources for gaining ongoing exposure for your work.

❑ Check Offline Publications

If you have been sending out press releases and/or CDs for reviews to offline publications, use the free "clipping services" to see if your efforts have been successful. Excite and Northern Light are the most recent. More archive sites are listed in *Measuring Your Success*.

❑ Consider Paid Clipping Services

If you have a large budget, consider using clipping services, like CyberAlert, to monitor the Internet and other offline publications.

· Monitor Your Web Site Regularly

❑ Perform Backlink Checks

Look in your access logs for information on visitors to your site. Ask your web host provider for further help. Each system is slightly different.

❑ Monitor The Number of Visitors and Hits on Your site

How long are visitors staying? What pages are they accessing most? Are they finding the pages you want accessed the most? Are people going to your order page and then leaving your site? If so, your order page may be too confusing or hard to use. Make adjustments to your pages to reach your goal.

❑ Measure The Effectiveness of Your Site

A lot of traffic to your site will only do you good if you are selling CDs and getting email addresses. If everyone is just passing by, then you need to reassess your web site's effectiveness. If you can't find anything wrong. Contact us at MusicPromotion.net. We offer consulting services that will make your site have a stronger impact on visitors: webdesign@musicpromotion.net.

NOTES:

NOTES:

CHAPTER 16

Zen & The Art of Internet Promotion

Throughout the course of this book, we have been exploring how to get online and stay there. Hopefully you have learned that there is more to just being online and getting good search engine placement. Also, that it is necessary to your longevity online to seek out new resources for constant exposure. Don't do your "homework" once and expect long term results. That is because the Internet is dynamic and changes constantly. This leads us to the first rule of the Three Golden Rules of Internet Music Promotion.

The Three Golden Rules

Promotion is an ongoing process. It is important to spend a little time every week to educate yourself on trends. This is because an independent artist can implement new technology and redefine marketing strategies overnight. This is not a bad position to be in while the music industry is downsizing, fighting piracy and trying to gain a foothold online! Now, the second golden rule of Internet music promotion.

What works today may not work tomorrow. Learn the fundamentals of this book and put your own twist on them. Although you still want to submit to search engines, place songs in Meta Sites, etc., don't sit back fat and happy. Find new resources to exploit and build up your momentum. Otherwise, your career won't go where you want it to.

Every online company that has become successful never followed traditional business models. For example, Yahoo! keeps on top of the *Cyberheap* by constantly launching new features on their site like "My Yahoo!", daily news, free email, personal calendars, and even a credit card. They aggressively advertise offline with TV commercials, print ads, sell merchandise and display their logo during sporting events.

All of this comes out of careful monitoring of online trends and creating new methods of promotion to exploit them. Of course, you don't have to pour this kind of money into your web campaign, but you should come up with new gimmicks that build repeat visits and attract newcomers. As we've covered in earlier chapters, these can be in the form of contests, giveaways and merchandise.

What works for others may not necessarily work for you. There isn't a perfect formula to online marketing but there is a golden path. To keep you on the golden path, we have put together an invaluable resource to accompany this book - **http://IndiePromo.com**. IndiePromo.com empowers independent artists worldwide with free tutorials, publications, study materials, and informative articles by respected industry professionals. With the purchase of this book, you are entitled to a free limited membership, where you can download the latest updates to this book, including chapters, resources, and promotion techniques. This resource will ensure that you will fulfill the *Three Golden Rules of Internet Music Promotion* and further your career.

Even with the Three Golden Rules, it is still easy to get lost without an overall plan. Make sure that you read and understand the first chapter, *Creating an Overall Strategy* and use the checklists at the end of each chapter to chart your progress. Also, always keep in mind the following:

What a Web Site Should Do For Your Music Career

Simply put, a web site should be used to build your music career. Most of my clients, as a direct result of their web site, have seen an increase in sales, higher attendance at concerts, and a stronger interest by A&R reps. This is how they do it and so should you:

- **Online Community:** Focus on creating an online vibe about your music with your web site by encouraging fans to interact with you – i.e. sign a guest book or send email. Aggressively promote your songs through other forms of online media using your web site as the hub of activity.

- **Easy to Remember Web Address:** Try to keep your address as short and memorable as possible - *yourbandname.com* or *first-and-last-name.com*. Only use alphanumeric characters – i.e. numbers and letters. Any strange characters in your site address like hyphens (-), dashes (/), and tildes(~) make it difficult to communicate your site verbally, as well.

- **Offline Web Site Promotion:** All of your merchandise, literature and press kits have to have your easy-to-remember web address visible. Your CD should have the address clearly printed on the jewel case, insert, and CD.

- **Regular Email Announcements:** Use your email list to keep fans informed, offer specials and announce upcoming gigs. By doing this you will attract new fans through the "word-of-mouth."

- **Fast Loading Pages:** It only costs a moderate fee to have tons of space and fast web access. Make sure that your host provider is giving you the space you need with room to grow. Free web services and Online Services like GeoCities and AOL, respectively, will cause you more problems than they are worth down the road.

- **Prizes:** Offer special discounts and hold contests to attract fans at gigs and encourage regular visits to your site. No matter how trivial the prize is, people love getting stuff for free and will talk about it to others.

Most importantly, make sure that your web site doesn't sell you short. Follow the basic site architecture laid out in *Elements of a Successful Web Site*. If you don't have the skill to create a matching mood on your site for your music, you should seriously consider hiring a professional web designer.

NOTES:

Reality Check: Traffic Doesn't Mean Jack

Yeah! A lot of people are talking about you and visiting your site, but that doesn't mean a thing unless you are making sales. Just because they are passing through your site, it doesn't mean you are a success. You should be getting some return for your hard work. Your success is measured by income derived from your visitors. Whether or not they are buying directly from your site or not, is not the measurement of success. It is measuring that with the addition of your web site, your sales and income have increased! You can have a million people walk by or through your "store" but if they aren't buying anything, you are going out of business.

Online Issues

CHAPTER 17

Protecting Music Online

Not every aspiring musician is excited by the idea that music buffs can download their music or pirate it, without paying a dime for it. Why not? Major Labels have complete control of almost every distribution channel, the airwaves, and a ton of money for promotion.

Since you are most likely unsigned and don't have a label to help distribute your music, you will need to make some of your music freely available online – just like handing out sample tapes. You should think of placing your work online as getting radio airplay or MTV exposure.

How Piracy Can Work in Your Favor

Many artists avoid the Internet because they fear theft of their work. These fears are largely unfounded because they don't understand the potential for exposure. To put it simply, unless they are selling a ton of records and getting a lot of radio airplay, piracy is not an issue. Prince, the Beastie Boys and Trent Reznor are more likely to lose a mountain of money to MP3 pirate sites than the struggling artist. This is because most pirated songs are "ripped" from store-bought CDs! However, the real question for independent artists is, what are they willing to give up for some exposure?

What Are You Willing to Give Up?

The Internet is rich with opportunity. The problem is how do you get paid? How much of your music are you willing to give up? Remember earlier when I mentioned that putting your music online is akin to getting radio airplay? You have full control over your copyright as an unsigned artist. This means you can distribute and promote your songs any way you see fit. You have ultimate say in what is released and whether or not to give it away. For the major artist, it's a different story.

Initially the recording industry ignored the Internet and even discouraged its artists from using it to distribute songs. Tom Petty is an example of this situation. In early 1999, he was looking ahead when he released a track on MP3.com. After his label found out he had a free song available for download on the infamous "pirate site," they forced him to remove it. What they didn't know was that Tom received some 7,000 emails with contact information during the week his song was available for the taking.

Think about what this means. Tom now knows which cities 7,000 people live in. He could conceivably launch an email promotion campaign for every city he tours in with a personalized message. He could ask each fan to attend his concert; tell them where to buy tickets; plug special deals and merchandise on his web site; and encourage fans to spread the word.

If you are still worried about how to protect your music online, the next section will discuss ways to help protect your store bought CDs from getting pirated and techniques that will encourage fans to purchase your music. All without hampering the "wow" factor of your site.

How to Protect Your Music Online

As an unsigned artist, you have more control over what is released and what isn't, than if you were under a label. If you are still worried about pirates stealing your music, keep in mind that 99.9% of the music found on pirate sites are encoded from store bought CDs that feature major groups.

Online Pirates are not going to bother themselves with copying an unknown artist's audio files and making them accessible from the web. Their MP3 archives are like any other web site trying to get more traffic. They want to attract more visitors to their sites with well-known artists. Besides, if fans are stealing you blind, your promotion strategy must be working! Unless you are internationally distributed through thousands of stores, you have little to worry about in terms of blatant theft of your work.

Ultimately, you will never be able to completely protect your music from theft. However, one can take steps to discourage this activity. Use the following tips individually or in combination:

• **Only place part of a song or video online**.
   Just put the parts that you feel capture the idea or message you are trying to convey. You want to sell your work…so put enough to tantalize! Your musical

style will determine the length. A sixty-second snippet should be enough to cover an intro and chorus. Be sure to fade out the last three seconds to avoid clipping.

- **Do not allow visitors to download files completely before play back**.
  Stream them, instead (Review *How to Become a Multimedia Dynamo*). Downloading before play back can have two adverse affects. One, a web surfer doesn't want to wait for a file to completely download. Two, a surfer will have copies of your work on his/her computer. This may not seem an issue to some musicians but it could reduce return visits. Consider this, once a surfer has a sound file, he/she won't have to return to the original site to buy the song because they already have it on their system.

  On the other hand, you may want to have people download your songs in MP3 format and distribute them publicly. You decide what is best for you or what your concerns are. The point is, you have complete control over what is distributed from your web site. Until your album is in stores, you could use piracy to your favor. After all, the money you could loose from piracy will probably end up getting lost to your label

- **Ask for something in return**.
  Don't just give away your music. Ask downloaders if they would kindly drop you a line with a comment about your work. After all, your web site is supposed to generate interest. Why not encourage new listeners to become fans? You may find your email box full of new contacts to add to your newsletter.

- **Use RealAudio and MP3/Liquid Audio in tandem**.
  Many surfers don't want to wait for huge MP3's to download. A great trick is to make a sample of your work available through a streamed low quality RealAudio snippet. Then interested parties can download or pay for a higher quality MP3 / Liquid Audio file.

- **Use material that is not available on official releases**.
  The best way around theft online is to put material not featured on your official releases. Or you could go the other way and only release singles or the tracks that are best suited to radio airplay. Either way, do not put all of your songs on the web for consumption. This will make your work more valuable and encourages fans to purchase a full CD. Releasing mixes, outtakes, live recordings, etc.

to the Internet are a great way to pique interest in your CD. A&R Reps new to your work, will see that you already have some history behind you.

- **Register Your CD with CDDB**.

  CDDB is an online service called, The CD Database. Every popular software program that either plays CD's on a computer, "rips" songs from audio CDs or stores your MP3 song collection, connects to this database for information about the music CDs you put in your machine. The way it works is that the program reads the audio CD for its unique serial number and checks to see if there is an entry in the CDDB. If there is a match, then the player automatically fills in the album title, album name, and song information into your player.

  This service was originally created to make it easier for CD rippers to create meaningful file names and organize songs in personal MP3 libraries. It has since become *the* de facto standard in tracking CD access online.

  If your CD was manufactured – not burned in your personal computer – then it will have a unique serial number that you can register with CDDB. Whenever your CD is played in a computer or "ripped", CDDB will most likely know about it. Although this information is not publicly available, yet, you will be in a good position when it will. Visit the CDDB site to find out how to get into their system: **http://www.cddb.com**. Their guidelines are strict. Do not deviate from them.

- **ID your audio files.**

  Put information about you and your copyright into every audio file you distribute. Every audio format allows you to embed your name, song info, and copyright information into the audio file, with the software used to create it. RealAudio, QuickTime, MP3, Liquid Audio, Windows Media, and even WAV files can have embedded information. However, be careful with the MP3 format. The ID3 "tag" that embeds your song information is not supported by every player and is rejected by MP3.com's servers when you submit your music. So you will need "unmarked" versions of your MP3 files for their systems.

- **Register your Copyright**.

  It is still important to formally copyright your materials and place a notice in plain view: "© Copyright 2000 Your Band Name: All Rights Reserved." This shows that you mean business. Your audio files are considered a tangible representation of your work and thus protected automatically. Unless you register your copyright with the Library of Congress, you won't be able to collect any monies for damages if you have a prosecutable case! See the chapter on *Cyberlaw* to find out more.

The following chart will help you pick the right format in combination with the above techniques:

What Each Web-friendly Audio Format Does to Protect Your Music Online

Audio Format	Security	Compression	Expiration	Streaming	ID Information
MP3		✓			✓
Real Audio		✓		✓	✓
Liquid Audio	✓	✓	✓		✓
WAV					✓
Windows Media		✓		✓	✓

Digital Piracy – What You Really Have to Worry About

The record industry has reacted slowly to the Internet and as a result, lost major ground in the future of online distribution. Their delay has been due to concerns over digital piracy and how to develop technology to suppress it. This has opened the door for other competing audio formats, namely MP3.

The MP3 format is at the focal point of the debate. Mainly because it is the format of choice for online pirates. It also happens to be the format used by MP3.com, a legal outlet for independent artists to sell their music. The key issue is, the MP3 format doesn't provide any built in security features.

Digital Music Distribution

Michael Robertson, MP3.com's founder, was thinking ahead when he purchased the virtual domain name and used it to provide a legitimate service for artists. By doing so, he gave the industry a hard enough kick in the pants to realize that the Internet was more than just a "fad" and that indie artists have a strong voice.

MP3.com consumers can download the songs they want or have them burned onto a CD-ROM – like a custom mix - while artists earn 50% royalties. None of the Big 5 could match that with their best offer. The prospect of artists earning half of all sales was unheard of and tipped the ears of the record industry.

Even though MP3.com and the MP3 format have since gained legitimacy, there is still a problem that should concern unsigned artists and the Big Five, alike. The MP3 format has no built in features to prevent piracy or track downloads for revenue – i.e. barcodes, Sound Scan, performance royalties, etc.

Because the industry had no hope of developing any technology of its own, it decided to form a coalition to encourage members from the hardware, software and music industries to come up with a viable solution as soon as possible. But I'm getting ahead of myself. Here is the whole story…

SDMI Mission Force

The Recording Industry Association of America (RIAA), which acts as the legal interest group of the Big Five record labels, spear headed a bold attempt to control online piracy. Their mission was to stop online piracy and secure a digital process that would guarantee the collection and tracking of revenue online. They knew that time was short and acted quickly, perhaps rashly.

MP3.com did not invent the MP3 format nor holds any patents. However, they have not bothered to correct this misunderstanding.

In Mid 1998, the RIAA began their "clean up" operation by approaching web masters that operated sites distributing illegal copies of commercial songs with "cease and desist" letters. But for every site they managed to shut down, ten more would pop-up in defiance. Most of these pirate sites operated outside of the United States, making it impossible for the RIAA to forcibly shut them down.

Soon after in October, Diamond Multimedia (DM) announced its plans to manufacture and distribute its portable MP3 player, the Rio. In desperation, the RIAA filed an injunction against them by to tie up DM's manufacturing of the device in court. The courts eventually ruled the Rio fell under "fair use" as defined in the Home Recording Act (1992). Distribution resumed and similar products from other manufacturers soon flooded the market.

The clock was now ticking faster for the RIAA. Not only had they been unsuccessful in preventing online piracy and the release of the Rio, they had no product or digital distribution in place to compete with smaller upcoming music "store fronts," modeled after MP3.com.

In a last act of desperation, the RIAA formed the Secure Digital Music Initiative (SDMI). SDMI's goal is to develop technical specifications for securing music distribution across all platforms – software and hardware. Another major goal of SDMI is to protect the interests of music copyright holders by developing a system to mark recorded music with rights management data that can be recognized by all audio devices. They have laid out a plan that will be executed in two phases.

Players that support the Phase I specification, will be able to play music in most current formats, including both protected SDMI and open formats like MP3. Phase II of SDMI will establish a secure format, which uses watermarking technology to embed copyright and licensing information in the music itself. Phase II compliant players will be able to detect and reject any pirated music that was originally created in the secure format. Phase II devices will also be able to play older songs in unsecured formats like MP3 without any restrictions.

To fund SDMI's operation, a ten-thousand-dollar entrance fee into the coalition was established to gain access to the guidelines. Some 100 music technology, software, and hardware companies raced to pay the entrance fee, to name a few, AOL, IBM, Intel, Texas Instruments, Sony, Microsoft, Liquid Audio, and even MP3.com. In order for these companies to be endorsed by the music industry, the security measures in the guidelines must be supported in their proprietary products. The guidelines have since been made public. To see them for yourself and a current list of SDMI members, visit the RIAA's web site: **http://www.riaa.org**.

> The Home Recording Act was the same law that protected Philips in the early 1980's against a lawsuit from the Motion Picture Industry over the VCR. Ironically, the VCR has led to a multi-million dollar after market in video sales. I suspect the same will happen with the digital revolution brought about by the MP3 file format.

There is No Conspiracy

The formation of SDMI infuriated online pirates and independent artists. For artists, the debate over "industry control" became extremely heated. Many believe that the music industry is trying to stop online music distribution or that they want to control the "next" distribution channel.

This is completely the opposite of the RIAA's intention. In addition to hampering piracy, their real concern is tracking sales online for artists and performance rights societies. It is good business for them to do so. Look at it like this, if you are a member of ASCAP and your music is getting better play online than on the airwaves, the technology being put in place will allow you to collect what is rightfully yours. Everyone down the road will benefit from industry concerns, signed and independent, alike.

Down the Road

One of the most promising technologies to come out of the SDMI fold is Liquid Audio. With this format, any artist can use several levels of security in combination to prevent piracy and aid in sales, through a network of 350 (and growing) sites distributing music in this format.

Even though the Liquid Audio format has the full backing of SDMI and the Recording Industry, unsigned artists will benefit, as well. With Liquid Audio's encoding software, any artist can set the number of times the file can be played back before "dissolving." Once the file dissolves, a "buy now" banner activates. An artist can customize the banner to point the listener to their site's order page or to any affiliate that carries the song.

The artist can also set a flag before the encoding process to disallow copying the file or burning it to a CD. This offers a level of security and potential source of revenue that independent artists were unable to gain access to. In addition, Liquid Audio Network will be used to track "webcasts" or "performances" to collect royalties for the performance right societies and to feed information to the charts! This means that Billboard Magazine may have Internet charts soon!

Still, hackers can and will eventually figure ways around the Liquid Audio encoding process. But as fast as hackers can break the code, software developers can release new versions! This will help the industry keep on top of piracy in an unprecedented way, while protecting the rights of all artists.

Piracy and the Technology Developed to Help Suppress It

Many record companies are hesitant about releasing songs in an open format like MP3 because of the potential for piracy and loss of revenue. As a result, several members of SDMI have developed secure music distribution systems designed to track downloads and prevent unauthorized copying. Watermarking and Encryption are the two most promising technologies that have emerged.

Watermarking

Watermarking transparently embeds copyright and licensing information into the music data of your audio file. Additional information can be stored in the file such as lyrics, album graphics and promotional material. This digital "signature" makes your audio files unique.

SDMI requires that all "secure music distribution systems" must use watermarking. Liquid Audio has broken significant ground in this technology, while other companies are competing for industry favor. Still, there isn't a firm standard in watermarking, yet. Visit these sites to find out more about this emerging necessity:

Liquid Audio – http://www.liquidaudio.com
Encoding.com – http://www.encoding.com.
Recording Industry Association of America - http://www.riaa.org

However, watermarking is only half the battle. Watermarked files are then encrypted and stored on a server with a database that tracks the number of copies transmitted and the amount of royalties due.

Encryption

Most secure music distribution systems use some form of encryption to prevent unauthorized use of songs. Some of these systems assign the "owner" of a song a personal key, which can only be used to "unlock" all the songs purchased by that user. Others require a separate key for each song. In each case, the consumer must use a software or hardware player supported by the system.

Other systems allow users to burn one copy of each song to a standard audio CD. However, there is nothing to prevent them from extracting the audio from that CD into an decrypted format that can be used anywhere, like MP3 or WAV files. Unless all the manufactures agree on a common format or "player," all encryption will do is make it difficult for fans to hear music. Unfortunately, encryption can not prevent a determined person from decrypting and copying the songs they like most, and it certainly is not going to stop bootleggers from pirating CDs; but it is a start in the right direction towards ensuring your royalties are collected.

CHAPTER 18

Music and the New Cyberlaw

Even though the Internet is only several years old, your basic rights as an artist are protected. This can be accredited to the emerging field of law referred to as Cyberlaw. Interestingly, the government has taken measures to avoid interfering with the rampant growth of commerce online by passing laws that place a moratorium on further taxation and creating new laws to help prosecute online offenders of copyright violation.

In this chapter, we are going to explore some of these laws, what your rights are, what others can and can't do with your work. In addition, we will discuss what to look out for with labels, webcasters, publications and artist directories. Let's begin with your basic rights as a copyright holder.

Miranda is Not Your Next Door Neighbor

Basic copyright law was officially extended into the online realm with the passing of the Digital Millennium Copyright Act; essentially making digital audio files a tangible form of expression for your work. This means that once your work is recorded to a digital audio file, it is automatically protected. A "tangible form of expression" is when your work is either recorded, written down on paper, printed in sheet music, or exists in any other medium considered fully expressed or realized. Still, Cyberlaw is in its infancy and it is important to understand what your exclusive rights are:

Your Five Exclusive Copyrights

- **Distribution:** The right to distribute copies of your work to the public by sale, lease, rental or loan.

- **Public Performance:** The right to recite or perform your work in a public place or transmit it to the public.

- **Public Display:** The right to show a copy of your work in a public place or transmit it to the public.

- **Reproduction:** The right to copy, duplicate, transcribe or imitate your work in a fixed form

- **Modification:** The right to modify your work or create a new work based on your existing work.

In short, you have the right to publish, distribute, publicly perform your work, authorize others to exercise your rights, and giveaway your rights. The right to publish means, you can decide whether or not to release a song, give it to the public domain, or to make money off of it – i.e. collect royalties. The right to authorize means, you can allow others to distribute your work. Your right to perform means, you can authorize others to perform your work and that you can it perform publicly.

Just as important, you also have the right to do none of the above. Most importantly, you have the right to authorize others, either in full or in part, to any of the above rights. This is where record deals come in. Typically, you give up a great deal of these rights so that the label can take your work and make some money with it. At least, that's the idea.

Why It Is Important to File Your Copyright With the Library of Congress

Your work is copyrighted as soon as it is in a "tangible form of expression." Technically, you don't have to register your copyright with the government. However, if you want to pursue any copyright violations of your work and collect damages from a lawsuit, you must register your copyright with the Library of Congress' copyright office. The so-called "poor man's copyright" of sending yourself a certified-mail package of your work does not hold up in court. This is because the court recognizes the sovereignty of the Library of Congress not Joe Blow Musician, as the self-appointed registration clerk.

In addition, now that you are on the Internet, it is extremely important that you register your web site itself, with the Library of Congress. Just as your songs are an important representation of your work, so is your site. At the very least, place your copyright "notice" at the bottom of each web page with an email link: "© Copyright 2000 Your Band Name: All Rights Reserved."

The phrase "All Rights Reserved." means that you and only you, may exercise the five basic copyrights covered above. It also identifies you as the sole entity to contact whenever a need for your material arises. It also let's everybody know you mean business.

Even though the Law no longer requires you to place a notice of copyright, you won't leave anything open to interpretation.

Any theft or unauthorized use of your materials may not be a concern of yours, but for larger artists, publicity is at the core of everything they do and needs to be tightly controlled and monitored by their label. By exercising their rights as copyright holders, labels can ensure that only the best representation of their artists' work will get exposure and that royalties will start coming in.

More Laws to Help Artists Flourish and Protect Their Work Online

There have been many other laws passed to protect the interest of the artist and to encourage the growth of online commerce - a.k.a. e-commerce. They range from what is considered fair use of your work to allowing the Internet to operate as a tax free zone. Most importantly, the passing of the Digital Millennium Copyright Act in early 1999 makes webcasting, digital audio files, and web sites tangible forms of expression, along side traditional offline media. Let's take a quick look at this law and how it relates to the basic Copyright Act and some of the new generation laws that enforce your rights on the Internet.

U.S. Copyright Act, Title 17

The Copyright Act gives artists the exclusive rights on copying and distributing their music. The artist may permit copying and distribution of their work and are entitled to royalties for that permission. This law limits public performance and broadcasting of copyrighted music by consumers, radio, television, and businesses.

Audio Home Recording Act of 1992

The Audio Home Recording Act allows consumers to record music for private, noncommercial use. If you're making money by playing or distributing copyrighted music, you must have permission, in the form of licensing, from the copyright holder. However, it is possible to obtain a blanket license from Performing Rights Organizations, instead of each individual artist.

Digital Millennium Copyright Act

In 1998, this act was put in place to make it illegal to make copyrighted music available online, for unlimited distribution without the permission of the copyright holder. This act also extended the scope of the U.S. Copyright Act to cover the Internet. It also clarified that online services and host providers could not be held responsible, for any material stored on their systems violating copyright laws. Instead, individuals that deliberately use these services to distribute copyrighted material are directly responsible. The Digital Millennium Copyright Act also puts specific limitations on the length of public broadcasts and on the types of song and artist announcements, that may be used with copyrighted music. These are covered later in the RIAA *Webcasting Criteria*.

Digital Performance Rights in Sound Recording Act of 1995

This law provides the copyright owner of a sound recording, the exclusive right to perform the recording publicly, by means of a digital audio transmission. It allows for transmission of copyrighted material within a business or within the immediate vicinity of that business. The act also allows copyright owners to negotiate and receive royalties for the use of that work.

First Sale Doctrine

The First Sale Doctrine is a portion of the U.S. Copyright Act where anyone who purchases a recording may then sell or otherwise dispose of that recording. However, the seller may not keep, sell or give away any other copies of said recording. In other words, if only one copy of a recording was purchased, then only one person should possess the original and any copies.

No Electronic Theft Act

The No Electronic Theft Act of 1997 amends the U.S. Copyright Act to define "financial gain" to include the receipt of anything of value, including the receipt of other copyrighted works. This means that a fan cannot give away your work even if money didn't exchange hands. They also can not claim that they didn't "know any better." The lawsuit against Naptser.com by the Record Industry is one of largest cases where this law empowered prosecutors. It also protects the interests of all artists online and offline.

What Major Labels Can't and Won't Do For Their Artists Online

Most of the major labels have not yet approved of distribution online because of concerns over piracy and tracking revenue. This poses a problem for major artists because they have "sold" their rights or "control" of their music to the label they are signed with. This situation is starting to slowly change as some of the majors are allowing promotional songs in MP3 to be made available through highly visible web sites.

In the meantime, if you are about to be signed, even to an independent label or a subsidiary of a major, ask what their policy is towards the Internet and if they will put promotion dollars into it. Otherwise, when you sign on the dotted line, you will be giving away some key rights that allow you to have control over your online destiny. You could inadvertently cripple your online exposure if your label doesn't want anything to do with or doesn't have the resources to use the Internet for exposure of your work.

Keep in mind that promoting your music online may be a conflict of interest in the eyes of your label. If your potential label isn't keen on the Internet, demand that a clause be added to your contract clearly stating who is responsible for promoting you online and/or offline. It also wouldn't hurt to ask for an "online" budget. "Zero Dollars" is a telltale sign that promotion on the Internet is not going to happen. Remember, you have the right to sign away all or some of your rights. By pursuing a special clause in your contract to cover the Internet, you will be able to hold on to the rights necessary to gain control of your promotion campaign online.

Many of the existing major artists are already up against the same wall – a fearful and slow to act record label. Remember the Tom Petty story in *Protecting Music Online*? He is a perfect example of what happens when your rights are in the hands of a label that discourages its artists from using the Internet. However, as time goes by, this attitude will change. The first sign of this was the merger, in early 2000, between AOL and Time-Warner.

Signing On the Virtual Dotted Line: What You Have to Look Out For

Because of the Copyright Act, web masters must obtain permission from the copyright holder of a song in order to place it on their site. This means that you or your agent/label will have to authorize any person or entity online for distributing your work. If you are asked to sign anything, make sure that you are only giving authorization to distribute your work and not giving away all of your rights.

Many of the larger artist directories, like MP3.com, are actually very flexible. By using their site, you agree to authorize them to distribute your song through their web site and a compilation CD if any of your work is selected. They also allow you to break the contract at anytime. However, online record labels are a different story. Be sure that you are not asked to give away any rights for an unreasonable amount of time, i.e. forever or a number of years. You should have the same expectation of a traditional record label. The only difference here is the medium through which your work will be gaining exposure and generating royalties. Not only that, the "digital millennium" has only just begun. There are sure to be changes and developments into "unknown areas" in the upcoming years. Signing away your rights now, could effectively end your career.

How to Avoid Webcasters That Could Hurt Your Exposure

The distribution of illegal copies of songs and transmission of pirated works has been a thorn is the side of The Recording Industry Association of America (RIAA) - the legal interest group of the Big Five record labels for the last few years. In an attempt to remove this thorn, the RIAA has created a set of criteria that webcasters must follow in order to be licensed or have the "blessing" of the industry. This is a good thing. Webcasters who follow these criteria will gain popularity on their own merit. This will ensure that your songs will be collecting royalties and generating other revenue through your site.

Let's take a look at what Internet radio sites to avoid because they violate the following criteria as listed on **http://www.riaa.com/newtech/dcma.htm**:

Sound Recording Performance Complement:
A webcaster may not play in any three-hour period more than three songs from a particular album, including no more than two consecutively, or four songs from a particular artist or from a boxed set, including no more than three consecutively.

Prior Announcements Not Permitted:
Advance song or artist playlists generally may not be published. However, webcasters may announce the names of a few artists to promote the type of music played on the site or channel. If an artist's name is announced, the webcaster may *not* specify the time that artist's songs will be played.

Archived, Looped & Repeated Programming:
Programs that are performed continuously, automatically staring over when finished, may not be less than three hours in duration. Merely changing one or two songs does no meet this condition. Additional parameters for these types of programming are set by the license.

Obligation To Identify Song, Artist, & Album:
Beginning October 1999, when performing a sound recording, a webcaster must identify the sound recording, the album and the featured artist. (Don't we wish that traditional broadcast radio falls under the same criteria!)

Other Conditions:
In addition to the above, webcasters must meet other conditions such as accommodating technical measures, taking steps not to induce copying and not transmitting bootlegs.

These criteria may sound harsh, but an advantage is created for independent artists here. More programming has to be rotated and more unique songs must be played during any programming period. This means that any legitimate Internet Radio site or webcaster that follows these criteria is more likely to be starved for music to play on their "shows." Make sure that they are also licensed by the Performance Right Organizations (PRO)! Otherwise, you are less likely to collect royalties from any airplay that you receive.

Incidentally, Internet Radio is still widely unmonitored by PROs. Write your PRO requesting that they add any of the sites that you get airplay on to their sample list, even if the webcaster has a blanket license. After all, you hired the PRO to monitor the media and collect royalties on your behalf. Hold them to it.

Conclusion

Now that you've read this book, spend some time to carefully develop your promotional plan. Remember, the Internet is not a replacement for traditional promotion, i.e. networking with people, gigging, handing out tapes, etc. It is merely a new medium at your disposal for enhancing your offline success, while your web site is the hub from which you run your promotional campaign.

When developing your plan, always keep in mind what your web site should do for your career – increase interest and CD sales. This is accomplished through fostering the "community feeling" on your site and making it as effortless as possible for fans to reach you and to purchase your work, i.e. a link to your order page and contact information on every page of your site, an up-to-date events calendar with directions and ticket information, and your web address imprinted on all literature and merchandise. Also, keep in mind the different needs and interests of your audience - fans, A&R reps, and the press. Otherwise, you could damage your online "persona" or prevent it from blossoming.

With a well-developed plan, you can easily measure your success and find the methods that work best for you. As soon as you get results, multiply your success by repeating the methods that worked best for your songs, by finding similar resources to exploit using the same methods. However, if you experience lack of interest, flat sales or even scathing reviews, your plan will help you to determine where you fall short and enable you to improve or remove the aspects of your campaign that cause harm to your online presence.

Feeling Overwhelmed?

My goal in writing this book is to empower you with the techniques you need to take control of your online presence. I took extra measures to ensure this, by including the comprehensive checklist to help you develop a solid plan, and to keep you focused on the aspects that have the highest return for your hard work. I've done my best to include every aspect of Internet promotion I could think of to make your campaign a success.

However, I know that the Internet is constantly changing and presents new opportunities everyday. To combat this, Tim and I have put together a companion web site for this book – http://IndiePromo.com – where you can get free updates to chapters and the checklist, more tutorials, study materials, resources, and promotion tips. See the coupon at the back of this book to find where to get your personal access code.

Now it's up to you to take your online presence to the next level. So go out there and give it your best shot. And when you do, drop me a line to let me know. If you have specific questions about your web site or how to promote it, fill out the "Free Consulting Services" form in the back of this book and send it in. I'll do my best to respond within three weeks of receiving your inquiry. (For the fastest reply, be sure to include your email address.)

Thanks, and best of luck to your career!

John Dawes

SECTION VI

Appendices & Resources

Comprehensive Checklist

CHAPTER 1 - 3:
Elements of a Successful Web Site

Check off all of the materials you already have and make notes on what you need. If you plan to have your site designed by a professional, skip the *Get Online* section and continue on to *Start Thinking About Your Image*:

- ## Gather Personal Information

    ❏ Compile Discography / Time Line

    ❏ Draft Bio
    > Avoid opening phrses like, "At an early age..."

    ❏ Draft Press Release
    > Prepare an announcement for the launching of your web site

    ❏ Gather Press Clippings & Reviews
    > If you don't have Reviews or Clippings, you'll have to send out CDs for review. See *Internet Radio & Online Publicity* for a ton of resources.

    ❏ Compile Gig Information
    > List your recurring gigs first. Then, list ALL of your gigs together. Don't forget directtions, contacts, and where to buy tickets!

    ❏ Consider Merchandising
    > Set a budget for T-shirts and stickers, at the very least. You can cut corners on T-shirts buy placing your web address on the left sleeve, instead of the front and back.

• Get Online

❑ Choose An ISP Based on Need:
How much room? (greater than 30MB is ideal)
Dial-in Access
Service / Customer Support
Web Server Features:
1 Personal Domain Name
2 Interactive Forms (CGI/Perl)
3 Email Account
4 SSL Encryption Server

- Free ISP's do not include 1, 2, 4, customer service, dial-in access, and provide little space (3 – 10MB)
- Commercial Online Services (AOL, etc.) typically only include 2, 3, and provide little space.
- Most Web Host Providers include 1 to 3. 4 is usually extra when available. Try to obtain a provider with at least 30MB housing space.

❑ Find a Web Designer or DIY
Get a Package Deal - Bio, Discography, Web Site Submission, etc.
- or -
Do It Yourself. You'll need to know:
HTML Programming
Multimedia Conversion
Graphic Design
FTP / Telnet / Maybe some UNIX
CGI and Perl scripting for forms
Web Page Optimization

• Start Thinking About Your Image

❑ What Image Do You Want to Present?

❑ Content and Layout?
Photos? Do I have all of the following ready: Bio, Press Release, and Reviews? Interactivity: Sign-In, Order, and Feedback forms? Do I want to publish a news-letter.

❑ **Color Scheme?**
    Avoid using pictures for your background. Only use solid colors. Remember, simple is better.

❑ **Logo?**

- **Consider Accepting Credit Cards**

Compare the Cost of the Following Methods:

❑ **If You Have Good Credit & Sell Tons of Your Music**
    Obtain a Merchant Account at a local bank

❑ **If You Have No / Bad Credit & Are Just Starting Out**
    Obtain Internet Billing - CD Baby - www.cdbaby.com

CHAPTER 4
How to Become a Multimedia Dynamo

- **Convert Your Press Kit to the Web**

❑ **Scan Album Covers Into Your Computer**
    If you don't have a scanner, your local copy center will have the facilities to help you.

❑ **Scan Photos Into Computer**
    Remember, only use professionally take photographs. Pictures taken a gigs by fans or amateurs will detract from you professional facade.

❑ **Scan Reviews & Clippings Into Computer or Place Quotes**
    Strip your reviews and clippings down to the "bones." No one wants to read the collective writings on your entire career. Highlight the good parts and edit out the rest. One to three lines, with the publication's name, will be plenty.

❑ **Enter Bio and Press Release into Press Kit Page**
    Don't forget to create a separate optimized page for A&R reps, the press, and your fans.

• Convert Your CD to Web-Friendly Formats

❏ **Download and Install "Ripping" Software on Your Computer**
RealAudio, MP3 are the most widely used formats online. Review *Web-Friendly Music Formats* to download the appropriate software.

❏ **Convert your Tracks to MP3 and RealAudio**
Create Meta Files (.ram) for RealAudio files to take advantage of streaming. See *How to Make RealAudio Stream From Your Site.*

• Put Your Music Files on Your Web Site

❏ **"Upload" or Send Your Files To Your Web Site**
If you don't know the first thing about transferring files from your computer to your web site, visit Newbie-U to take their tutorial on "FTP" - http://www.newbie-u.com. By the way, FTP stands for File Transfer Protocol.

❏ **"Link" To Your Music Files To Your "Audio Samples" Page**
Build a web page for your music samples with URLs pointing to each audio file on your web site. Then, upload or "send" the "audio samples" page to your web site.

❏ **Test Streaming Audio and Other Formats**
Visit your web site's audio samples page and click on the links to make sure that your RealAudio files stream and MP3s download properly. Remember, you need RealPlayer or any MP3 players installed on your computer, in order for sound to work properly from your site. Make sure that visitors are notified which audio formats each URL points to.

CHAPTER 5
Starting a Propaganda Machine

• Raise Awareness Offline

❏ **Join An Organization**
A great way to meet new people and gain more resources. There are also online organizations to join. You have no excuses to avoid networking! See *Networking* to find out where you can meet more people online and offline.

❑ Send Press Kit and Releases

Start with the local press and balloon out statewide and then regionally and eventually nationally. See next chapter on how to create appealing press releases.

❑ Update Literature & Merchandise

Everything you own should have your web address on it.

❑ Alternate Forms of Promotion

Stickers, Posters, Postcards are more affordable that you think!

CHAPTER 6
Using the Press to Your Advantage

- **Draft Press Release In Established Format**

❑ Catchy Headline

Pique your audience's interest with a short catchy headline.

❑ Provide Facts in the Body

Give a brief description of your news worthy item and then back it up with facts.

❑ Contact / Booking Information

This is the perfect opportunity to take advantage of free advertising for your web site.

❑ End the Release with 3 Pound Signs: ###

This signifies THE END!

- **Draft A Cover Letter**

❑ Get the Name of the Contact

Contact the media you are interested in submitting your material to and get a contact name. Important!

❑ Customize Your Letter For Each Contact

Do not address your letters "To Whom It May Concern". Use the name of the individual that has final say in releasing your material

❑ Include Your Events Calendar

If the publication is in your local area or has a representative nearby, they may send somebody over to your show to observe your talent for later review in their publication.

· **Draft A Biography**

❑ A Bio Can Be Used Instead of a Press Release

A bio can be used when nothing new is happening with your music, but you still want to get the word out.

· **Gather More Media Contacts**

❑ Find Ezines That Cover Your Genre of Music

Between MediaFinder, Band Utopia, Indie Music, and IndiePromo.com you will cover a lot of online and offline territory. They all have online searchable databases for offline publications.

❑ Fanzine or Music Scene Rags

No matter where you live there are always local music scene publications! When you tour, find publications that cover the area you will be gigging in and send your press materials.

❑ Gale Directory of Publishing & Media

Visit your local library and do some research. You can find TV and Radio Stations, magazines, and newspapers. This is only a last resort.

CHAPTER 7
Using Email Effectively

· **Generate Initial Traffic To Your Site Through Email**

❑ Create A Signature File

With a signature file configured in your email and newsgroup programs every post and email you send will have your essential contact information - email, URL, and Band Name. You can go as far as to place a couple of your upcoming shows into your signature file.

❏ Draft Your "Arrival on the Web" Announcement for Existing Fans

Keep it short and to the point. Word it so that visitors will know why they should visit your site. Just try to pique interest; don't give the hard sell. Try offering something free or have a contest of some sort.

❏ Email Existing Fanbase

If you don't have any email addresses of your fans, start collecting them at concerts. If you don't gig…start gearing up for the rest of your promotion campaign.

❏ Grow Your Own Email List

Try to make giving an email address the easiest and quickest thing visitors can do on your site. By doing this early on, you are preparing your site for the new fans arriving at your site, generated by your promotion efforts.

CHAPTER 8
Understanding Search Engines

WARNING: Do not do any of the following until your web site is finished! Otherwise your search engine placement will be adversely affected. *Never* submit an incomplete site or one under construction!

• **Optimize Your Site For Every Search Engine: Deep, Directory, Human Driven**

❏ Select A List of Keywords

Your keywords should embody your musical style, abilities, name, influences and the instruments you play.

❏ Prioritize Your Keywords

Reorder your list based on how you want to market your abilities. Try to have unique keyword tags in every page.

❏ Make Your Keywords Plural

Make each word in your list plural. Some surfers search on the plural of a word.

❏ Consider Misspellings

If a word in your list is commonly misspelled, add it. For example "Web Design" is often misspelled as *"Web Desgin."*

❑ **Test Your Keywords**
Visit all of the major search engines and perform a search on your top words. Visit the top listings and view their HTML code for the keywords that got them to the top. You may find more applicable words to your site. Don't paste or add their list into your HTML code. Be unique!

❑ **Place Your Final Keyword Choices**
Put your keywords in order of importance on a single line in your HTML documents. All of the popular WYSIWYG web page editors take care of this for you.

❑ **Write <META> Descriptions**
Write a different description for each page on your site. These are to be placed in the <META Name="description" Content="your description here!" > tag. Deep Search Engines use this tag to describe your page to visitors. WYSIWYG editors are helpful here, too.

❑ **Use Top Keywords in <TITLE> tags**
Write a unique title for each page on your site. These are to be placed between the <TITLE> & </TITLE> tags. Most search engines use this as the clickable link to your site. See example next page.

❑ **Try To Use Top Keywords in <BODY>**
Insert your most pertinent keywords into your page content. The heading tag enforces the importance of the words for some search engines - <H1> & </H1>, etc.

NOTE: http://www.webreference.com has a tutorial that can explain all of those <xxx> & </xxx> thingies. Since HTML programming is easily a subject for another book we recommend that you make use of their free tutorials.

CHAPTER 9
Submitting to Search Engines

• **Double Check Every Page**

❑ **Make Your Keywords "Fit" Each Page**
"Tune" each page for the intended audience - fans, press, A&R reps - by reordering or adding keywords.

❑ **<META> Description Says "WHY"**
Word your description to say why surfers should drop by - free music, contest, etc.

❏ <TITLE>s Read Like a Headline

A Title is displayed in most search engines first like a newspaper headline. Write your titles in the same manner.

• **Submit To The Top Six Deep Search Engines**

❏ AltaVista

www.altavista.com/av/content/addurl.htm

❏ Lycos

www.lycos.com/addasite.html

❏ Infoseek

www.infoseek.com/AddUrl?pg=DCaddurl.html

❏ Excite

www.excite.com/info/add_url

❏ Hot Bot

www.hotbot.com/addurl.asp

❏ Web Crawler

www.webcrawler.com/Help/GetListed/AddURLS.html

• **Prepare Descriptions For Other Engines**

❏ Subject Specific Directories

You will have to manually enter the Title and Descriptions in your META tags with these search engines. Save yourself some work by keeping your titles, descriptions, and keyword lists in a text file. This will enable you to cut and paste them in Directories and Human Driven Engines.

❏ Yahoo! (Covered In Next Chapter) and the Open Directory

Same deal here. I know it sucks....but the mice are separated from the men this way.

❏ Save In Plain Text File For Later Use

Add what you submitted to your plain text file.

- **Submit To Subject Specific Directories**

  ❑ Music Yellow Pages
  www.musicyellowpages.com

  ❑ MuseNet
  www.musenet.com

  ❑ Search for More Music Related Sites
  There are more in the *Internet Resources* section. Once you have exhausted the list, go to your favorite search engine and do a search.

CHAPTER 10
To Yahoo! or Not to Yahoo!

- **Create A Page Designed To Yahoo!**

  ❑ Find the Appropriate Category
  Search on your keywords to find a category that suits you **and** your site. Click on the category and look at listings to get the "vibe." Click on AddURL graphic to begin submission process

  ❑ Find An Alternate Category
  Search on your other keywords to find more categories.

  ❑ Use Keywords in URL
  Based on your primary category, create directories on your site and place your Yahoo! enhanced HTML document there. For example, your category is composer: *www.myband.com/music/composer/yahoo.html*. This will help the Yahoo! staff place your site correctly.

  ❑ Draft A One Line Description
  Your <META> description is not used by Yahoo! So you will have to draft a short 25 (or less) word statement that tells surfers why they should visit your site.

- **Submit Your Special Page to Yahoo!**

  ❑ Try the Main Directory
  Sit back and wait for a few weeks. You may not get added. Remember, 70% of all submissions are denied.

❏ Try the Local Directory
   If a few weeks go by and your submission is not in Yahoo!, try the "local" Yahoo! listings. They have one for most metropolitan areas.

❏ Try Events
   If you're still not getting in, you can squeeze in the back door, especially if you are a part of a onetime or seasonal event.

❏ Try Try Again
   Still didn't make it? Hone your site and make it better! Try all over again!

CHAPTER 11
Where Does the Money Come From?
No Check List
If You Haven't Already, Start Putting Together Your Plan of Attack!

CHAPTER 12
CyberPrise: Thinking E-Commerce

• **Place Your CDs Into Key CyberSpace Depots**

❏ CD Baby
   www.cdbaby.com

❏ The Orchard
   www.theorchard.com
   Decide whether you want them to distribute to Amazon.com, CDNow, and Music Boulevard for you, or go to them individually to provide your music with the expanded look and feel that you want

• **Place Your Hit Songs Into Online Stores & Meta Sites**

❏ MP3.com
   www.mp3.com

❏ Rolling Stone Magazine
   www.rollingstone.com

❑ Stompinground.com
www.stompinground.com

❑ Liquid Platinum (350+ Online Stores for $99/yr!)
www.liquidmusicnetwork.com

❑ Find More Online Stores & Meta Sites in Search Engines

- **Place Your Hit Songs and Information Into Artist Directories**

❑ The Ultimate Band List (UBL)
www.ubl.com

❑ Internet Underground Music Archive (IUMA)
www.iuma.com

❑ IndieGroup
www.indiegroup.com

- **Find an Internet Record Label That Fits Your Promotion Campaign**

❑ AMP3.com
www.amp3.com

❑ Emusic.com
www.emusic.com

❑ Find More Labels in Search Engines and at IndiePromo.com
Remember, you can "sign" with as many record labels as you like, as long as you don't give away all of your distribution rights. Make sure you know what you are getting into before you sign anything.

- **Adopt A Business Model For Selling CDs & Merchandise Direct From Your Site**

❑ Pick One
Free Song + Upgrade
Trial CD Offer
Subscription – offer this only if you have a large and extremely loyal fan base

CHAPTER 13
Internet Radio and Online Publicity

- ## Make Sure Your Online Press Kit is Ready for Prime Time

  ❏ ### Double Check Your Materials
  Make sure that your site communicates clearly how to contact you and where to go get more info for write-ups. In the event you are contacted by editors or program managers, always be professional and prompt in your replies!

- ## Draft An Email "Cover Letter" For Contacting Station Managers

  ❏ ### Keep Your Correspondence Professional and to the Point
  Avoid a "desperate" tone of voice in your letter. You want to come across as a confident veteran of the industry. Don't forget to include the URL for your online press kit.

- ## Draft Newsletter For Potential Exposure Gained

  ❏ ### Include News, Discounts on Merchandise and CD, & Events Calendar
  When the publicity flood gates start to open, your new fans will want to know everything about your latest ventures. Having a newsletter ready to roll will save you the headache of growing pains and show that you are a true professional.

- ## Get Your CD Reviewed

  ❏ ### Submit Your CD to the more reputable Review Sites
  www.demorama.com, www.cdreviews.com, www.indiepromo.com/reviewers

  ❏ ### Find Ezines to Review Your CD and Write-up Your Act/Site
  Visit UBL and BandUtopia to find publications that cover your genre(s). Don't forget local music scene sites in your "sphere of influence" and in areas that you tour. Also, be sure to refer to the Ezine resources table in *Internet Radio & Online Publicity: Ezines*.

  ❏ ### Contact Every Applicable Ezine You Find
  Remember, approach Ezines like you would any other high-profile media. Unless a publication expressly permits it, do not send any pictures, songs, or press materials with out their permission first.

- **Begin Penetrating Internet Radio Based On Success with Reviews**

  - ❏ Find Reputable Internet Radio Stations
    Visit the MIT Radio Directory, the Online Radio Directory, and IndiePromo.com's list of stations looking for submissions. Before submitting any material, be sure that the station is:

    1. Licensed with your Performance Right Organization.
    2. Has you sign a distribution agreement, not all of your rights away.
    3. Has DJ's or a Programming manager so you can forge a relationship.

  - ❏ Contact Appropriate Sites
    Describe your music and include your URL to your press kit page. If you are a crossover artist, ask where you fit into their programming. You may get several songs on different programs!

- **Integrate Your Site With Any Exposure Gained**

  - ❏ Place Write-Ups from Reviewers & Ezines in Your Newsletter & Site
    Don't forget to link back to the site or publication that reviewed you!

  - ❏ Link to Radio Stations That Are Giving You Airplay
    Don't forget:

    1. D.J. or Station Manager email links for requests.
    2. Broadcast range and Station ID (freq. and call letters) for offline stations.
    3. URL to Page on Internet station where your hit song can be heard.

CHAPTER 14
Covering Your Bases

- **Generate More Traffic To Your Site**

  - ❏ Create A Signature File If You Haven't Yet
    With a signature file configured in your email and newsgroup programs, every post and email you send will have your essential contact information - email, URL, and Band Name.

❑ **Draft Your Announcement**

Keep it short and to the point. Word it so that visitors will know why they should visit your site. Just try to pique interest; don't give the hard sell. Try offering something free or have a contest of some sort.

❑ **Find Applicable Newsgroups To Promote Your Site**

If you can't find any decent groups through your local ISP, use DejaNews to do a search and post your announcements. Remember, newsgroups are not a good place to promote your CD! Only use them to promote your site! Follow the examples on how to draft your message.

❑ **Find Applicable Email Lists**

Look at the table of resources for a starting point.

❑ **Grow Your Own Email List**

Try to make giving an email address the easiest and quickest thing visitors can do on your site. Having a clickable button that automatically sends you an email address is the simplest solution.

• Generate Online Awareness

❑ **Ask Web Masters For Tips**

Visit your favorite web site and ask their web masters for tips. Web masters love adoration.

❑ **Start Researching Web Rings**

Find the best Web Ring that suits your site, i.e. specific genres, interest, instruments, etc. Visit www.webring.org to search their index.

❑ **Awards**

See the table on Award resources to find an appropriate award for your site. Try to shoot for high-profile awards and then work your way down the "totem pole" to the lesser known awards.

❑ **Find Other Sites to Swap Links**

Swap only with professional looking sites. Stay on the topic of music. Create a "how to" page for fans to increase the incentive.

❏ Consider Banners As A Last Resort

Avoid using other banners on your site if at all possible - i.e. only distribute yours. Banners only do a site good if there is already a lot of traffic. Before you consider using them, grow you traffic by traditional means - i.e. search engines, announcements, email, etc. If you join a banner exchange program, place any banners deep within your site - i.e. sub-pages like your guest book, after an order has been submitted, etc.

CHAPTER 15
Measuring Your Success

· Monitor Search Engines

❏ Check Your Keywords' Effectiveness

Use TrackerLock and the other services outlined in *Measuring Your Success*.

❏ Check Newsgroups for Buzz About You

Use DejaNews to search on your name or band, or to find any potential resources for gaining ongoing exposure for your work.

❏ Check Offline Publications

If you have been sending out press releases and/or CDs for reviews to offline publications, use the free "clipping services" to see if your efforts have been successful. Excite and Northern Light are the most recent. More archive sites are listed in *Measuring Your Success*.

❏ Consider Paid Clipping Services

If you have a large budget, consider using clipping services, like CyberAlert, to monitor the Internet and other offline publications.

· Monitor Your Web Site Regularly

❏ Perform Backlink Checks

Look in your access logs for information on visitors to your site. Ask your web host provider for further help. Each system is slightly different.

❑ Monitor The Number of Visitors and Hits on Your site

How long are visitors staying? What pages are they accessing most? Are they finding the pages you want accessed the most? Are people going to your order page and then leaving your site? If so, your order page may be too confusing or hard to use. Make adjustments to your pages to reach your goal.

❑ Measure The Effectiveness of Your Site

A lot of traffic to your site will only do you good if you are selling CDs and getting email addresses. If everyone is just passing by, then you need to reassess your web site's effectiveness. If you can't find anything wrong. Contact us at MusicPromotion.net. We offer consulting services that will make your site have a stronger impact on visitors: webdesign@musicpromotion.net

APPENDIX B

Internet Resources

QUICK REFERENCE GUIDE

Visit: http://IndiePromo.com/checklist to update this section.

Web Site Resources

Internet Service Providers
The List – Where to find ISPs   http://thelist.internet.com

Web Host Providers
Top 25 Web Host Providers   http://webhostlist.com
Search and Compare the Top WHPs   www.tophosts.com

Domain Name Registration
Network Solutions   www.networksolutions.com

Web Page Editors
DreamWeaver   www.macromedia.com/dreamweaver
Visual Page   http://shop.symantec.com/trialware
Netscape Composer   www.home.netscape.com
More Places to Check   http://builder.cnet.com/Authoring/Htmleditors

Web Site Utilities
TagMaster   www.tagmaster.com
Web Site Garage   www.websitegarage.com
Web Monkey   www.webmonkey.com

Forms, Chat, Guestbooks, Scripts, Etc.
Matt's Script Archive   www.worldwidemart.com/scripts
Java Script Source   www.javascriptsource.com
WebResource.net   www.webresource.net

Software Resources

CD Rippers and Audio Encoders
RealAudio:
    RealJukebox   www.real.com
    RealProducer   www.real.com

Liquid Audio:
    LiquidPlayer   www.liquidaudio.com

MP3:
    MusicMatch   www.musicmatch.com
    Audio Catalyst   www.audiocatalyst.com
    RioPort   www.rioport.com

Macromedia:
   Shockwave   www.shockwave.com

WindowsMedia:
   Netshow   www.windowsmedia.com

QuickTime:
   QuickTime Audio   http://quicktime.apple.com

Graphic Utilities
FireWorks2   www.macromedia.com/fireworks
Paint Shop Pro – JASC Inc.   www.jasc.com

Sound Utilities
GoldWave   www.goldwave.com
Cool Edit Pro   www.syntrillium.com
Shareware Machine   www.hitsquad.com/smm
Harmony Central   www.harmonycentral.com

Search Engine Resources

The Top Deep Engines
AltaVista   *http://altavista.digital.com/av/content/addurl.htm*
HotBot   www.hotbot.com/addurl.asp
Lycos   www.lycos.com/addasite.html
Infoseek   www.infoseek.com/AddUrl?pg=DCaddurl.html
Excite   www.excite.com/Info/add_url.html
Web Crawler   www.webcrawler.com/Help/GetListed/AddURLS.html

The Top Human Driven Engines
About.com   www.about.com
The Open Directory   www.dmoz.org
Yahoo   www.yahoo.com/docs/info/include.html

Specialty Search Engines To Find Music Related Search Engines
Beaucoup   www.beaucoup.com
Argus Clearinghouse   www.clearinghouse.net
TheBigHub   www.thebighub.com
FinderSeeker   www.finderseeker.com

Meta Search Engines – Search Multiple Engines With These
DogPile   www.dogpile.com
MetaCrawler   www.metacrawler.com

Visit: http://IndiePromo.com/checklist to update this section.

MetaFind	www.metafind.com
Savvy Search	www.savvysearch.com
SuperSeek	www.superseek.com

Automated Services That Monitor Your Search Engine Placement

TrackerLock	www.peacefire.org/tracerlock
The Informant	http://informant.dartmouth.edu
URL-Minder	www.netmind.com/html/url-minder.html

Song Distribution Resources

Affiliates

| Liquid Platinum | www.liquidmusicnetwork.com |

Meta Sites

MP3.com	www.mp3.com
Riffage	www.riffage.com
Rolling Stone Magazine	www.rollingstone.tunes.com
StompinGround.com	www.stompinground.com

Artist Directories

IUMA	www.iuma.com
UBL	www.ubl.com
IndieGroup	www.indiegroup.com
More Places to List Your Band	www.musicyellowpages.com
	www.taxi.com
	www.tourdates.com

Internet Record Labels

AMP3.com	www.amp3.com
Emusic.com	www.emusic.com
SpinRecords.com	www.spinrecords.com

E-Commerce Resources

Drop Shippers
CD Baby	www.cdbaby.com
CDNow	www.cdnow.com
Amazon.com	www.amazon.com
The Orchard	www.theorchard.com/index1.html

Internet Billers
CCNow	www.ccnow.com
IBill	www.ibill.com
ClickBank	www.clickbank.com
Spyro	www.spyro.com
ValidCheck.com	www.validcheck.com

Credit Card Processing Services
Card Services International	www.cardservices.com

Magazines and Ezines of Interest

Quick Reference of Online Publications Accepting Press Releases
Addicted to Noise	www.addict.com/ATN
All Star Magazine	www.allstarmag.com
Billboard	www.billboard.com
Electronic Musician	www.emusician.com
Film Music Magazine	www.filmmusicmag.com
Gajoob	www.gajoob.com
Gavin	www.gavin.com
Getsigned	www.getsigned.com
Gig Magazine	www.gigmag.com
Guitar	www.guitarmag.com
Guitar World	www.guitarworld.com
Keyboard	www.keyboardmag.com
The Island Ear	www.islandear.com
Mix	www.mixonline.com
Music Connection	www.musicconnection.com
Music Dish	www.musicdish.com
Music Maniac	http://music.maniac.com
Pollstar	www.pollstar.com
Rolling Stone	www.rollingstone.com
Talk Music	www.talkmusic.com
Vibe	www.vibe.com
WebNoize	www.webnoize.com
Wired	www.wired.com

Visit: http://IndiePromo.com/checklist to update this section.

"Human Networking" Resources

Places to Find Organizations

Jeff Mallot's Songwriter Site	www.lyricist.com
Muses Muse	www.musesmuse.com
IndiePromo.com	http://IndiePromo.com/orgs

Offline Publication Resources

Music Related Publication Resources

Band Utopia	www.bandutopia.com
Indie Music	www.indie-music.com
IndiePromo.com	http://IndiePromo.com/ezines

Publication Search Engines

MediaFinder	www.mediafinder.com
News Paper Assoc. of America	www.newspaperlinks.com
College Newspapers	www.cpnet.com
MediaINFO Links	www.mediainfo.com/emedia
NeWo News	http://newo.com/news
Gebbie Press	www.gebbieinc.com
NewsDirectory.com	www.newsd.com
ARJ NewsLink	http://ajr.newslink.org
News365	www.news365.com
PubList	www.publist.com
World Press and Media Finder	www.escapeartist.com/media/media.htm

Press Release Utilities

MediaMagnet	www.mediamagnetpro.com

Press Release / Newswire Services

Collegiate Presswire	www.cpwire.com
Eworldwire	www.eworldwire.com
PR NewsWire	www.prnewswire.com
URL Wire	www.urlwire.com
NetPOST	www.netpost.com
Internet Media Fax	www.imediafax.com

More places to find targeted press release services
   http://dir.yahoo.com/Business_and_Economy/Companies/Communications_and_Media_Services

Online Publication Resources

Publication Search Engines

News Paper Assoc. of America	www.newspaperlinks.com
College Newspapers	www.cpnet.com
MediaINFO Links	www.mediainfo.com/emedia
NeWo News	http://newo.com/news
Gebbie Press	www.gebbieinc.com
NewsDirectory.com	www.newsd.com
ARJ NewsLink	http://ajr.newslink.org
News365	www.news365.com
PubList	www.publist.com
World Press and Media Finder	www.escapeartist.com/media/media.htm

Clipping Services and Archive Resources

Free Tools for Searching Offline Publications

Excite's News Tracke	http://nt.excite.com
Norhtern Light	www.northernlight.com/news.html

Places to Search Archives

Hot Bot: News Channe	www.newsbot.com
Newshub	www.newshub.com
TotalNEWS	www.totalnews.com
News Hunt	www.newshunt.com

Ezine Resources

Reviewers

DemoRama	www.demorama.com
CD Reviewers	www.cdreviews.com
IndiePromo.com	http://IndiePromo.com/reviewers

Ezine Search Engines

Ezine Seek	www.ezineseek.com
Info Jump	www.infojump.com
News Resource	http://newo.com/news

Visit: http://IndiePromo.com/checklist to update this section.

Ezine Directories

The Ultimate Band List	www.ubl.com/magazines.asp?mode=genre
John Labovitz's Ezine List	www.meer.net/~johnl/e-zine-list
Ezine Adsource	www.ezineadsource.com/d6pages/div6main.htm

Internet and Broadcast Radio Resources

Internet Radio Sites That Accept Submissions

AudioNet	www.audionet.com
Green Witch	www.greenwitch.com
House of Blues	www.hob.com
LiveConcerts.com	www.liveconcerts.com
RadioTV	www.radiotv.com
World Music Radio	www.worldmusicradio.org

Radio Directories

MIT Internet Radio Directory	http://wmbr.mit.edu/stations
IndiePromo.com IR List	www.indiepromo.com/ir
Radio Directory	www.radiodirectory.com/Stations

Newsgroup Resources

Comprehensive Lists of Newsgroups

Internet FAQ Consortuim	www.faqs.org
Liszt	www.liszt.com/news
Tile.Net	www.tile.net/news
Usenet Info Center	http://metalab.unc.edu/usenet-i
Yahoo! Newsgroup Listings	

http://dir.yahoo.com/Computers_and_Internet/Internet/Usenet/Newsgroup_Listings

Newsgroup Search Engines

DejaNews	www.dejanews.com
RemarQ	www.remarq.com

Public News Servers

More places to find public news servers

http://dir.yahoo.com/Computers_and_Internet/Internet/Usenet/Public_Access_Usenet_Sites

Mail Lists and Discussion Group Resources

Some Great Places to Find Discussion Lists
OneList	www.onelist.com
EGroups	www.egroups.com
Topica	www.topica.com
Publicly Accessible Mailing Lists	www.neosoft.com/internet/paml

"Early" Internet Discussion List Resources
ListServ	http://scout.cs.wisc.edu
New-List	www.new-list.com
Tile.Net	http://tile.net/lists
Vivian Neou's List of Lists	http://catalog.com/vivian
Liszt	www.liszt.com

Web Site Awards

The More Reputable Award Sites
Project Cool	www.projectcool.com/sightings/
USA Today Hot Site	www.usatoday.com/life/cyber/ch.htm
Yahoo! What's New	www.yahoo.com/picks
NetGuide Internet Site of the Day	www.netguide.com

Sites That Track Lesser Known Awards
Award Sites!	www.awardsites.com
Web Site Awards	http://websiteawards.xe.net

Also, search on "music web site awards" in your favorite search engine.

Legal Resources

Performance Right Organizations
ASCAP	www.ascap.com
BMI	www.bmi.com
SESAC	www.sesac.com
Peermusic	www.peermusic.com
NMPA	www.nmpa.org
EMI	www.emimusicpub.com

Copyright & Publishing
Copyright Office	http://lcweb.loc.gov/copyright
Music-Law.com	www.music-law.com
Musician's Law	www.musicianslaw.com

Visit: http://IndiePromo.com/checklist to update this section.

Glossary of Terms

- A -

Access provider
Organization that arranges for you to have access to the Internet through a dial-up account. The charge is usually depending on the amount of usage you contract for.

Ad
A graphic or a banner on a web page that when clicked on, takes the visitor to another site.

Ad Click
A click on an advertisement on a web site which takes a user to another site.

Ad View
A web page that presents an ad. Once the visitor has viewed an ad, he/she can click on it (see Ad Click). There may be more than one ad on an ad view.

Applet
Small (Java)program embedded in an HTML page. When you access that Web page, the browser downloads the applet and runs it on your computer. For security reasons applets cannot read or write data onto your computer. The applet can only be executed if your browser supports Java.

Authentication
Technique by which access to Internet or Intranet resources requires the user to identify himself or herself by entering a username and password. A.k.a "logging in."

- B -

Bandwidth
Measure (in kilobytes of data transferred) of the traffic on the site.

Banner
Advertisement in the form of a graphic image on the Web. Most banner ads are animated GIF's.

Bookmark
Browser feature that allows you to save a link to a Web page. You can always use this bookmark to return to that page.

Bounce
Return of an email because it could not be delivered to the specified address.

Browser - Web Browser
A program used to locate and view HTML documents (Netscape, Mosaic, Microsoft Explorer, for example.)

Byte
A set of 8 bits that represent a number from 0 to 255.

- C -

cc:
Carbon Copy. To send somebody a copy of an email message.

CGI - Common Gateway Interface
Interface that allows scripts (programs) to run on a Web server. CGI-scripts are used to put the content of a form into an email message, to perform a database query, to generate HTML pages on-the-fly, etc. The most popular languages for CGI-scripts are Perl and C.

cgi-bin
The most common name of a directory on a Web server in which CGI-scripts are stored.

Chat
Online interactive communication on the Web. You can "talk" in real time with other people in the "chat room," but the words are typed instead of spoken.

Click -through Rate
Percentage of users who click on a viewed advertisement. This is a good indication of the effectiveness of this ad.

Client
The browser used by a visitor to a Web site.

Client Errors
An error occurring due to an invalid request by the visitor's browser. Client errors are in the 400-range. See "Return Code" definition.

Commercial online service
Computer network that offers its members access to its own chat rooms, bulletin boards, and other online features on a monthly fee basis. Well-known commercial online services are America Online, CompuServe, The Microsoft Network, and Prodigy.

Compression
Technology that reduces the size of a file to save bandwidth.

Cookie
Persistent Client-State HTTP Cookies are files containing information about visitors to a web site (e.g., user name and preferences). This information is provided by the user during the first visit to a Web server. The server records this information in a text file and stores this file on the visitor's hard drive. When the visitor accesses the same web site again, the server looks for the cookie and configures itself based on the information provided.

- D -

Data encryption key
String of characters used to encode a message. This encoded message can only be read by someone with another related key.

Dial-up
Temporary connection (over a telephone line) to the computer of your ISP in order to establish a connection to the Internet.

Discography
A musician's full catalog of works. Usually a listing of an artist's recordings in chronological order.

DNS - Domain Name Server or Domain Name System

A Domain Name Server maps IP numbers to a more easily remembered name. When you type http://www.indieguide.com into your browser, the DNS (specified when you installed dial-up networking) searchs for a matching IP address (209.32.201.64). If the DNS doesn't find an entry in its database, it will ask other DNSs until the entry is found, and you will see our site. Otherwise, you'll get an error message from your browser.

Domain name

A unique name that identifies an Internet site. A domain name points always to one specific server while this server may host many domain names. If you look at the URL for this page, you'll see www.indiepromo.com at the beginning. The "www" points to the server and "indipromo.com" is our domain name. Most domain names are assigned by the Network Solutions (a.k.a. InterNIC.) They can be reached at www.networksolutions.com. The fee for owning a domain name is currently $70 for the first two years, and $35 a year thereafter. Domain name purchasing is first come first served.

Download

Transfer of data from a server to your computer's hard disk. You can use your browser or an FTP program to download files to your computer. When you're retrieving your mail, you're downloading your mail to your computer.

- E -

Email - electronic mail

Message, usually text, transmitted over the Internet and sent from one person to another (although you can also sent email to a large number of email addresses (mailing list)).

Email address

An electronic mail address. Email addresses are in the form of: user@domain (for example: info@indiepromo.com).

Encryption

Procedure that scrambles the contents of a file before sending it over the Internet. The recipient must have software to "decrypt" this file. If you want to transmit "hot stuff" like credit card information or a password, you have to use some form of encryption. PGP (Pretty Good Privacy) is a commonly-used encryption program. SSL (Secured Socket Layer) is a commonly used encryption on the Web to transmitted information submitted by users on a web site's form.

- F -

FAQ - Frequently Asked Questions

Document that contains the most common questions and answers on a particular subject.

Filters

A means of narrowing the scope of a report or view by specifying ranges or types of data to include in or exclude.

Flaming

A highly evolved and impersonal form of punishment - electronic scolding - for those that do not obey Netiquette. Usually accomplished by nasty email and newgroup replies. Newbies are the the most common victims. See spam and newbie.

Forms
An HTML page which passes variables back to the server. These pages are used to gather information from users. Also referred to as scripts.

FTP
File Transfer Protocol is a standard method of sending files between computers over the Internet.

- G -

GIF - Graphics Interchange Format
Common graphics file format on the Internet. This format can display only 256 colors at the maximum (8 bits), therefore a GIF is mostly used to show clip-art images (photographic images are usually in the JPEG format). The GIF 89a standard allows multiple images in one file, so you can use a GIF file to show some animation on your Web site.

Gigabyte
About 1 billion bytes.
1 Kb = 1,024 bytes
1 Mb = 1,024 Kb (= 1,048,576 bytes)
1 Gb = 1,024 Mb (= 1,073,741,824 bytes)

- H -

Hit
A single request from a browser to a server. Some servers also count each graphic on that page as a hit. For this reason, it's doubtful to use the number of hits as an accurate measurement for the popularity of a Web site.

Home page
The main page of a Web site. The home page provides visitors with an overview and links to the rest of the site. It often contains or links to a Table of contents for the site.

Home Page URL
The local path or Internet URL to the default page of the Web site browers access, i.e. **http://www.indiepromo.com**.

Host
The server on which a Web site is stored.

HTML - Hypertext Mark-up Language
The coding language used to create hypertext documents on the World Wide Web. HTML is a way to format text by placing marks ("tags") around the text (like old-fashioned typesetting code).

HTTP - Hypertext Transfer Protocol
The World Wide Web protocol for moving hypertext (HTML) files across the Internet.

Hypertext
Text that includes links to other Web pages. By clicking on a link, the reader can easily jump from one Web page to another related page. Hypertext spins the Web, without hypertext no Web!

- I -

Impression
Each request for a Web page on a particular

server. These days, most server log files only count impressions, not "hits" (which may include requests for graphic files). Counting the impressions is a good way to measure the popularity of a Web site. See Visit.

Indie
Independent. As slang term to describe an unsigned musician or band.

Internet Explorer
Web browser from Microsoft.

InterNIC - Internet Network Information Center
The InterNIC is the entity that keeps track of the domain names. Most domain names are registered with the InterNIC. A.k.a. Network Solutions.

IP Address
Internet Protocol address identifying a computer connected to the Internet.

ISP - Internet Service Provider
An "ISP" provides Internet access to its members. Every time you log on, your ISP connects you to the Internet.

- J -

Java
A platform-independent programming language invented by Sun Microsystems that Web developers use to create applets (see applets). Java-enabled Web pages can include animations, calculators, scrolling text, sound effects and even games. Although many Web designers like Java because of its possibilities, they have to take into consideration that many people are surfing the Web with a Java disabled browser, simply because they don't want to wait until some applet is entirely loaded into their browser.

JavaScript
JavaScript is a scripting language unrelated to Java, designed by Netscape. JavaScripts are embedded into HTML documents.

JPEG - Joint Photographic Experts Group
Image compression standard, optimized for full-color (millions of colors) digital images. You can choose the amount of compression, but the higher the compression rate, the less quality the image has. Almost every full-color photograph you see on the Web is a JPG file, while GIFs are used to display clip-art images (up to 256 colors).

- K -

Kbps - Kilobits per second
Measure of data throughput. A 28.8 Kbps (kilobits not kilobytes!) modem transfers data at about 3.6K (kilobytes) per second.

Kilobyte
Rounded: a thousand bytes. Actually, 1024 (2^{10}) bytes.

- L -

Link
Marked text (usually underlined) or picture within a hypertext document (Web page). With just one click of your mouse, a link brings you to another Web page (or to another place on the same page). Links are essential in hypertext

documents, without links one can hardly speak of "hyper"text.

Location
Internet address as displayed on your browser. When you type in the URL of a Web site into the location bar of your browser, your browser will take you to this page.

Log file
File that contains recorded events of a computer system, e.g. server access log files, error log files etc.

Login
Entering into a computer system. Also the account name (or user ID) that you must enter before you can have access to some computer systems.

- M -

Mailing list
Email based discussion group. List servers maintain a list of email addresses of subscribers. When you send an email message to this group, your email is copied and sent to all subscribers.

Mail server
Server of your ISP that handles incoming and outgoing email.

Megabyte
About one million bytes. Exactly 1,048,576 bytes (2^{20}), or 1,024 Kb.

Modem
Contraction of MOdulator-DEModulator. A modem allows computers to transmit information to each other via ordinary telephone lines.

MP3 or MPEG 3
Compression standard for music. Although the compression rate may be very high, you'll have almost no loss of quality. This makes it a very attractive method to copy CDs. It's no wonder that the music industry is not very happy about these MP3 files...

MPEG - Moving Pictures Expert Group
Compression standard for video in a format similar to JPEG.

- N -

Navigator
Web browser from Netscape.

Net
Short for Internet.

Net surfing
Browsing the World Wide Web, without a specific goal in mind.

Netiquette - Network etiquette
Informal code of good manners on the Internet.

Netizen
A responsible citizen of the Internet.

Netlag
Condition that occurs on the Web when heavy traffic slows down server response time.

Newbie
Someone that is new to the Internet and is immediately fingered out by "stupid" questions and *flames*.

Newsgroup

Discussion group (on USENET) among people who share a mutual interest. In one particular newsgroup you can find several conversations ("threads") on different (to the newsgroup related) topics. There are thousands of newsgroups, covering almost every possible subject.

NNTP - Network News Transport Protocol

Protocol to transport USENET postings over a TCP/IP network.

- O -

Offline

Not connected to a computer network.

Online

Connected to a computer network.

- P -

Page

Shortening of "Web page" (one single file on the Web).

Page Views

Also called Page Impressions. Hit to HTML pages only (access to non-HTML documents are not counted).

Password

Secret code that you must enter after your user ID (login name) in order to log on to a computer.

Perl - Practical Extraction and Report Language

Perl is a powerful computer language, especially used for writing CGI scripts which handle input/output actions on Web pages.

Platform

The operating system (i.e. Windows 95, Windows NT, etc.) used by a visitor to your Web site.

Plug-in

Small piece of software, usually from a third party developer, that adds new features to another (larger) software application.

POP - Post Office Protocol

Internet protocol used by your ISP to handle email for its subscribers. A POP account is just a synonym for an email account.

Posting

A single message posted to a newsgroup, bulletin board or mailing list.

Protocol

An established method of exchanging data over a network or the Internet.

- Q -

Query string

Your input to a server on the Internet. For example, when you perform a search on a search engine.

- R -

Referrer
URL of an HTML page that refers to your Web site. See Link.

Return Code
The return status of the request which specifies whether the transfer was successful or not and why.

Possible "Success" codes are:
```
200 = Success: OK
201 = Success: Created
202 = Success: Accepted
203 = Success: Partial Information
204 = Success: No Response
300 = Success: Redirected
301 = Success: Moved
302 = Success: Found
303 = Success: New Method
304 = Success: Not Modified
```

Possible "Failed" codes are:
```
400 = Failed: Bad Request
401 = Failed: Unauthorized
402 = Failed: Payment Required
403 = Failed: Forbidden
404 = Failed: Not Found
500 = Failed: Internal Error
501 = Failed: Not Implemented
502 = Failed: Overloaded Temporarily
503 = Failed: Gateway Timeout
```

Router
A router sends data packets back and forth between networks.

- S -

Search engine
Web site that allows users to search for keywords on Web pages. Every search engine has its own strategy for collecting data, so it's no wonder that each search produces different results

Server
A computer that has a permanent connection to the Internet. The purpose of a server is to supply information to client machines. A typical use of a server is to provide Web site housing and access.

Server Error
An error occurring at the server. Web server errors have codes in the 500 range. See Return Code.

Sig - signature file
A small ASCII text file (four or five lines only), automatically attached to the end of an email message that includes additional information about the author.

Site
A place on the Web. Refers to a home page or to a collection of Web pages.

SMTP - Simple Mail Transfer Protocol
Main protocol to send and receive email between servers on the Internet.

Snail mail
Regular postal mail. Refers to its slowness in relation to electronic mail.

Spam
Junk email. Spam is considered a serious breach of netiquette.

Spider
A small piece of software that trolls web sites for key information that search engines use for indexing.

SSL - Secure Sockets Layer
Protocol that allows sending encrypted messages across the Internet. SSL uses public key encryption to pass data between your browser and a given server (for example to submit credit card information).

Streaming audio/video
Technology that allows to play audio or video while it is still downloading.

Suffix (Domain Name)
The three digit suffix of a domain can be used to identify the type of organization.

Possible "Suffixes" are:
  .com = Commercial
  .edu = Educational
  .int = International
  .gov = Government
  .mil = Military
  .net = Network
  .org = Organization

Surfing
Browsing the Web, just looking around.

- T -

TCP/IP
Transmission Control Protocol/Internet Protocol - Known as the language if the Internet.

Computers on the Internet talk to each other using this language.

Telnet
Internet protocol that lets you connect your machine as a remote terminal to a host computer somewhere on the Internet.

Time out
When you request a Web page and the server that hosts the Web page doesn't respond in a certain amount of time, you may get the message "connection timed out."

Triple-dub
Abbreviated way to say "www" when reciting a URL.

- U -

Upload
Sending files from your computer to another computer through the Internet. For example, sending email is uploading a file to the SMTP server of your ISP. When you have a personal home page, you must upload your HTML files to the Web server that hosts your Web site.

User Agent
The fields in an extended Web server log file indicating the browser and the platform used by a visitor.

URL
Universal Resource Locator is a means of identifying an exact location on the Internet. For example, http://www.indiepromo.com/web/stuff/index.html is the URL which defines the use of HTTP to access the Web page Default.htm in the /html/info/ directory on the WebTrends Corporation Web site). As the pre-

vious example shows, a URL is comprised of four parts:

```
Protocol Type (http://)
Machine Name (indiepromo.com)
Directory Path (/web/stuff/)
File Name (index.html)
```

User Session
A session of activity (all hits) for one user of a web site. A unique user is determined by the IP address or cookie. By default, a user session is terminated when a user is inactive for more than 30 minutes.

Usenet
World-wide decentralized distribution system of newsgroups. Newsgroups (discussion groups would be a more accurate name) cover almost every human proclivity. No one can really count the number of newsgroups because not all Usenet machines are connected to the Internet, however, there are at least 30,000 newsgroups available through the Internet.

User ID
A unique identifier that you enter every time you want to access a particular service on the Internet. The user ID is always accompanied by a password.

- V -

VRML - Virtual Reality Modeling Language
Method for creating 3D environments on the Web. On a VRML page, it is possible to move around through a virtual room, pick up things, open a door etc. To see VRML pages, you need a VRML plug-in for your browser.

View, Page
Each request for a particular web page which displays an ad. Also referred to as an impression.

Visit
Commonly called User Session. All activity for one user of a web site. By default, a user session is terminated when a user is inactive for more than 30 minutes.

- W -

Webmaster
The person who is responsible for the Web server (usually the sysdamin.)

World Wide Web
An Internet client-server system to distribute information, based upon the hypertext transfer protocol (HTTP). Also known as WWW, W3 or the Web. Created at CERN in Geveva, Switzerland in 1991 by Dr. Tim Berners-Lee.

WYSIWYG
What You See Is What You Get. A phrase that is used to explain that what you see on the screen is what you will get on a print out.

- XYZ -

No Entries

- 0-9 -

No Entries

NOTES:

NOTES:

NOTES:

NOTES:

NOTES:

Free Consulting Services!

If you have specific questions you'd like to ask John Dawes about your web site or how to promote it, fill out this form and mail it in. However, with your full paid membership, you can contact him through the companion web site – **http://IndiePromo.com/membership**. (Please allow three weeks for a response. Only inquiries containing this form will receive a reply.)

Please Print Clearly

Your Name: _____

Name of Band: _____

Address: _____

_____

Phone: _____

Fax: _____

_____

Email Address: _____

Web Address: _____

_____

Questions: _____

_____

_____

_____

_____

_____

_____

_____

Mail to: **Free Consulting Services**
Taco Truffles Media
PO Box 500202
San Diego, CA 92150

How to Get Access to the Companion Web Site

With the purchase of this book, you get unlimited access to updates on:

- Chapters
- Study Materials
- Internet Resources
- Tutorials
- Promotion Tips
- and Informative Articles From Respected Industry Professionals

You also get a free limited-time membership to our "Indie Insider" section where you get access to:

- Personalized Consulting
- Audio Seminars
- Multimedia Tutorials
- Music Promotion Tool Kit
- Promotional Literature Samples
- Discounts on books, equipment, services and software
- and Insider Tips on the latest developments that effect your career

To get started right away, visit and login as:

http://IndiePromo.com/membership

Login: **indie**
Password: **power**

Don't delay your success any longer. Sign up now.

We've Got it Covered...

Between Tim Sweeney & Associates and Taco Truffles Media, your success is a sure thing. With our integrated services, your online and offline presence will work together to generate the most exposure possible for your music. Check out our list of services below:

Services Available from Taco Truffles Media & John Dawes:

- Web Design & Hosting
- Site Evaluation & Promotion
- Identity & Branding
- Multimedia CD-ROMs

Visit Taco Truffles Media on the Web today to experience our portfolio - **http://www.tacotruffles.com/webdesign** - or call for more information (858) 613-1635.

Services Available from Tim Sweeney & Associates:

- Artist Development
- Consulting
- Distribution Network
- Retail Marketing
- Publicity
- Radio Promotion
- Market Research

Visit TSA on the Web today - **http://www.tsamusic.com** - or call for more information (909) 303-9506.